Little Evil

Little Evil

Jens Pulver

with
Erich Krauss

ECW PRESS

Published by ECW PRESS
2120 Queen Street East, Suite 200
Toronto, Ontario, Canada M4E 1E2
416.694.3348 / info@ecwpress.com

NATIONAL LIBRARY OF CANADA CATALOGUING IN PUBLICATION DATA

Pulver, Jens
Little Evil: one ultimate fighter's rise to the top / Jens Pulver, Erich
Krauss.
ISBN 978-1-55022-567-9
1. Pulver, Jens. 2. Martial artists—United States—Biography.
I. Krauss, Erich. II. Title.

GV1111.P84 2003   796.815'092   C2003-902186-6

Acquisition and production: Emma McKay
Copy editor: Mary Williams
Design and typesetting: Yolande Martel
Third Printing: Thomson-Shore
Cover design and illustration: Jean Labourdette

This book is set in Janson and Univers

PRINTED AND BOUND IN THE UNITED STATES

ECW PRESS
ecwpress.com

*Dedicated to my mother and to all the coaches
who have guided me over the years.*

Contents

1

Day of the Gun

When I was seven years old, my father decided that he no longer wanted children. On a cloudy Seattle afternoon, he grabbed my two younger brothers and me by the collars of our shirts and hauled us into the living room. After lining us up in a little row by the fireplace, he stumbled into the kitchen to fetch his shotgun.

Dustin, Abel, and I knew what our father was planning to do, even though he hadn't spoken a word. Hearing him clatter through the broom closet in search of his misplaced weapon, I felt energy dancing in my fingertips and groin. This was the end of my life, the end of this pathetic excuse for a family. In just a few moments, there would be no more pain.

Never again would I have to listen to the man who called himself my father grunt and groan as he beat on my mother with his fists and feet in the middle of the night. Never again would I piss my pants when I came home from school and saw his car parked in the driveway. I wouldn't have to listen to his drunken speeches anymore, or feel his knuckles tear into me, creating wounds so deep they pulled me screaming from my dreams. The fear that inhabited every chamber of my mind was finally going to be silenced by its creator.

When my father stormed back into the living room, his eyes burned with a fury that I have not seen since, not in all the battles I've waged against opponents who tried to beat me within an inch of my life. He uttered not a single apology or explanation for the sin he was about to commit. He simply said, "I'm going to execute you all," with a coldness that can only come from a man too afraid to venture inside his own tortured soul.

Because I was the eldest, the one who always ran to defend our mother, he crammed the barrel into my mouth first. As urine soaked my jeans, I stared down the length of steel into my father's haggard face. What I would remember more clearly than my brothers' soft weeping or my mother's hysterical pleas was the reek of my father's breath. It stank of liquor and anger and failed dreams.

The father-son showdown seemed to last for hours. Although my eyes were as wide as the barrel pressing against the back of my throat, I tried not to focus on his callused finger slowly tightening on the trigger. I looked straight ahead, into his squinty eyes, and as I watched his fear of life contort his face and raise the veins in his neck, I knew he was attempting to summon one final ounce of drunken courage to get rid of his last responsibilities. I could feel the conflict that raged inside him radiating from his pores. He craved freedom from being a man—freedom from all things that could cause him to fail. All he really wanted to do was crawl into a hole in the ground and die, a bottle in his hand.

But my father proved to be a failure even at taking the lives of his boys. Perhaps he found a shred of love that hadn't been crushed out of him by his own violent father or destroyed through years of pissing away his talent as a jockey. Perhaps he saw a little bit of himself in me and remembered how free he'd felt as a child. But, looking back on that afternoon, I think that my father was just too afraid to finish something he'd started. When I close my eyes and recall the loathing on his face, I have no doubt that he simply wanted us gone, lying on the carpet with the color draining from our bodies. He just couldn't finish what he'd started, and back then it made me hate him even more.

"You aren't worth the bullets," he eventually said. Then he slowly pulled the barrel from my mouth. Out of that whole chaotic afternoon, those words were the one thing I never forget, even in my happiest moments. I, Jens Pulver, just wasn't worth the bullets.

A rusty taste lingering on my tongue, I watched my father turn away from us and head for the back-yard, mumbling that he was going to kill himself. My mother, who died a million deaths that day, pulled us to the floor, and there we huddled, listening for the blast that would end the terror. But although I wanted him gone, I did not wish him dead. He was still my father—the man who built up kingdoms then smashed them down with a swipe of his hand. In my small world, I still thought he had the right.

Waiting for the gunshot that would end the unbearable silence and my father's reign of terror was somehow more horrifying than waiting for him to put a bullet in my own skull. Even though I so young, I sensed that once he was out of our lives for good the true horror of what I'd been living though would set in. All the energy I'd harnessed for survival would be redirected into healing. I would have to look inside myself for the first time, and, scarred by years of abuse, I was afraid of what I might see.

When the shot finally rang out, it sounded like two trains colliding. It sounded like thunder. My mother's arms tightened around Dustin, Abel, and me, and she pulled our heads together until they were touching. At that moment, I was too exhausted to think about what this meant. I was too numb to contemplate our next move. For years I had been floundering in a stormy sea, and now the sea was suddenly calm. And although there were even darker clouds brewing on the horizon, I didn't attempt to swim to shore. If it had been up to me, I would have stayed on the living room floor for an eternity, curled up in my mother's arms.

But my father ruined that plan, just as he ruined everything else. Ten minutes after that liberating shot echoed through the house, I heard his boots scuffing across the kitchen floor. For a moment I thought it was just my mind refusing to accept that he was dead, but then I felt my mother trembling, and I knew that she'd heard him too.

When his swaying silhouette appeared before us, my eyes ran up and down his body, searching for a hole, a trail of blood. But he was as intact as ever, the same drunk father I had always known. And now he was even more furious than he'd been when he lined me and my brothers up in front of the fireplace. He was pissed because we hadn't gone out and checked on him, and he vented his anger on my mother the only way he knew how.

That's just how things were. My brothers and I grew up in a home where every day was a battle. We tasted fear every morning, afternoon, and night. We became so used to it that it became an addiction, and its influence was stronger than any drug sold on the streets.

Fear taught me how to fight with my fists. Fear taught me how to take charge and get what I wanted by whatever means necessary. Fear put me on the path to becoming a world-champion athlete, to proving wrong all those people who said I wouldn't amount to anything. And this path—which led me to become one of the most feared pound-for-pound cage fighters in the world—eventually enabled me to put childhood demons to rest and find inner peace.

But, as you will see, it was a long path to travel.

2

The Backside

Let me go back a little. I grew up in a five-bedroom, two-story rambler in Maple Valley, Washington, half an hour from Seattle. Our property was the kind most kids would kill to grow up on. We had horses running on an acre and a half of land that was so green you couldn't walk ten feet without hitting a tree. I knew there were plenty of neighborhood kids who envied the hell out of me, sitting up on that big old porch with my two younger brothers and baby sister. But if those kids had come closer—close enough to see what went on behind our closed doors—they'd probably have avoided the entire block, just like those kids in *To Kill a Mockingbird*.

Just down the street from our house was the Long Acres racetrack, which is where my father made most of his money—and for a while he made quite a bit of it. His only ambition growing up had been to ride horses competitively, and so the day he turned sixteen he became a licensed jockey. For eleven years he rode at Bay Meadows, Long Acres, Portland Meadows, and a dozen other West Coast tracks. He became known for his athleticism and his natural talent, and for a time he was considered one of the best jockeys in the business. Despite his flaws, I have to admit the man knew how to ride.

Horsemanship was in my father's blood. The men in his family tended to be small, and three generations of them had been riders. But along with inheriting the build of a champion racer, my father had inherited a talent for tipping the bottle. In the end, he turned out to be better at sitting on a bar stool than he ever was at sitting on a horse. And it was his undying love of alcohol that ended his riding career. To be a jockey, you not only have to be fit and nimble, but you also have to be light. A man who consumes five thousand calories' worth of booze every night before bed doesn't remain a lightweight for long. So when his weight became a problem, my father did everything he could—aside from sobering up—to shed those extra pounds. When starvation dieting didn't do the trick, he resorted to drugs. As you might imagine, that didn't add much joy to the family unit. How happy can an overweight jockey be when he's drunk, high on drugs, and dying for a burger—all the while watching his career spiraling down the drain?

Eventually my father was forced to stop riding competitively, and, like many athletes whose glory days have passed, he became a trainer. He expected his boys to help out, so while we were growing up, Dustin, Abel, and I practically lived in a Long Acres shed row.

Luckily for us, Long Acres was one of the most majestic racetracks in the country. It was built during an era when people were willing to spend a lot of money to create something beautiful. Stepping through its gates was like entering a magical kingdom, steeped in history. Sometimes, in the early morning hours, long before the crowds arrived, I'd climb into the bleachers to do some thinking. On more than one occasion, I swear that I could hear the hooves of long-dead race-horses pounding down the track.

My family rented one of the dozens of barns located in the back side of Long Acres, and for the first ten years of my life I considered Barn 23 to be my home. And what a home it was! We ran free in our own little wonderland. Every Sunday morning, the pastor would come around with his wagon to collect us for bible school. In October, my mother would decorate our place with carved pumpkins and plastic spiders, and for the month of December a holiday wreath would be nailed to the barn door. Every night, I went to bed with straw in my hair and dirt under my nails, my head full of the little adventures I'd had that day.

We worked as hard as we played. In the beginning, my father ran a tight ship. At four years old, I already had a feed bucket in my hand, and as I got older I started taking on more and more responsibilities. I lined the horses' stalls with straw, hooked the horses up to the exercise walker, and washed them. And when I was big enough, nine or ten years old, I began galloping horses. According to my father, we were going to be jockeys, and sometimes he'd make sure I was the first one on top of a new thoroughbred. I'd get bucked off and land with my face in the dirt, but I'd hop right back into the saddle. Despite smashing my head on a couple of occasions, I loved that part of living at Long Acres—being out there in the dirt and waking up every morning to the smell of horse shit.

There was a downside to being raised on the Backside, however: the seasonal workers. Just as there were winners and losers in the stands every night, there were winners and losers working behind the scenes. The winners, of course, were the trainers and the insanely rich racehorse owners who stopped by occasionally to see how things were going. The losers were the laborers who shoveled shit by my side each day for hours on end.

They weren't bad people; they were just totally uneducated. Most of them would likely have become carnies if they hadn't been raised around horses. They constantly came and went, in and out of jail, driven by their most primal instincts, telling tall tales about life on the road. Many of them blew every last cent of their hard-earned pay on alcohol and drugs, and when worst came to worst, they bedded down in the stalls, sleeping in the shit they would have to shovel out the next morning.

Now, I don't look down on these people, because I believe that each person has the right to choose his or her own path. But if you spend a lot of time around folks like this when you're just four years old, then you start to believe that their way of life is the only way of life.

I saw it happen a hundred times to kids just like me, kids being raised in the Backside. It wasn't uncommon for a twelve-year-old boy to walk around slinging a bottle of beer, talking like he was thirty-five. It wasn't uncommon to see a group of kids smoking cigarettes and playing poker in a dark corner. At nine years old, I chatted with ex-felons and watched illegal Mexican laborers scurry away every time they caught wind of a deportation raid. The Backside was a world of its own, a place where you grew up hard and fast. If you were a racetrack kid, you either loved it or hated it.

In my family, Dustin was the one who loved it, and he probably loved it even more than our father. He loved the horses, the betting, the drinking, the drugs—all of it. At school, he couldn't sit still for more than five minutes, and he didn't think he had any reason to. The track was where he received his education.

Some of Dustin's favorite times growing up were when my father dumped us off on a few of the older racetrack kids. At ten years old, Dustin would follow those boys around as if they were gods, sipping from a bottle of whiskey. He'd throw an arm around one guy's shoulders and talk about how he was going to conquer the world. He didn't weigh more than eighty pounds— he was just a hotheaded little scrapper, all skin and bones, but in his own mind he was larger than the troublemakers he revered. From them he learned marijuana, he learned cocaine, and he learned alcohol. As far as Dustin was concerned, the track was paradise.

Having such negative role models, Dustin headed

down a bad road at a very young age. Before he had even reached his teens, he'd made up his mind that he wanted to be a gangster when he grew up. He told our mother this one day when he was in the eighth grade, and he even demonstrated to her on paper how he was going to make a profit selling drugs. Although he was convinced he couldn't do math, if you asked him how many ounces were in a kilo he'd tell you right off.

Dustin knew what he wanted, and what he wanted was cars and guns and women. He wanted to wear medallions around his neck and to be respected like Al Capone. And the racetrack, a community filled with other boys who had similar aspirations, was a place where Dustin felt free to imagine a life of criminal splendor. Soon, the merest mention of the track would bring a sinister smile to his face, and even though I was still trying to make sense of the world myself, I knew that the Backside would be his demise. With every hour he spent there, I could see his ambitions burning brighter in his eyes, and I knew that he was searching for a way to make them a reality.

Each year, I saw Dustin slip further away from me, and it made me search even harder for a way out of the Backside. Although I loved the horses, loved the feeling of being out in the sun, it was all too easy for me to picture myself at thirty-five, a bottle in one hand and a horse brush in the other, searching the barns for an empty stall to rest my head. I was realistic enough to know that while some can make a life out of it, others get pushed under. They give in to darker temptations, and soon every day is a battle. At that point, I'd already battled enough. I just wanted to move towards a future that wasn't filled with pain.

For a time—I can't remember how old I was, maybe nine or ten—I'd gaze out my bedroom window every night at the Washington sky and pray for a miracle. Sometimes, my mother, Marlene, would come and sit by my side. She was a small lady, she didn't even weigh a hundred pounds, yet she carried a thousand pounds of pride. Her roots were Native American, and her hair was long and black and as smooth and thick as a thoroughbred's tail. When she looked at me with her loving brown eyes, I'd find myself wondering if she too was praying for the same miracle.

My mother loved her kids unconditionally, and she was a solid woman. Just one look at her weather-beaten face told you she was a warrior. But, like all warriors, she had one weakness: my father. Some people might think her pathetic for staying with a man who beat on her, but she wasn't concerned about her own physical safety—she was terrified for her kids. And she struggled to keep things together for us. Over the years, she worked herself to the bone, until three disks in her back just crumbled to pieces.

The life she had with my father was the only life my mother knew. After graduating from an all-girl Catholic high school, she had left home against her parents' wishes to discover the mysterious world of the racetrack. For her, the track wasn't about fancy dress, fame, or acquiring wealth. She was drawn to the track by her love of horses and her need to be around other people who had a similar passion. Since she'd been old enough to stand, she'd been in the saddle. While other girls she knew were interested in boys and college, Marlene was bent on learning to gallop, train, and break horses. Those four-legged creatures were the focus of her life, and when she arrived at Long Acres, she felt like she was in heaven.

Needless to say, when she met my father, a champion jockey at the height of his career, her interest was piqued. He courted her, and for months he was nothing but loving and devoted, but after Abel was born his bad side emerged. By then, however, Marlene was already trapped in the life they had made together. Whenever she talked about leaving, my father would torture her by saying things like, "If you ever leave me, I swear to God, I'll kill the kids." After the incident with the shotgun, I don't think she doubted his sincerity.

So we all did what we could to survive. My brothers and I went down to the track and worked our little butts off. We attended school and tried our best to avoid our father, but as time went on things seemed to be spinning out of control.

Then that miracle I had been praying for occurred—even though I didn't recognize it until later. It was our mother who dropped it into our laps, and, looking back, I guess it's safe to say that Marlene was the real miracle.

3

On the Mat

The summer before I was to enter the sixth grade, my mother took me, Dustin, and Abel down to Tillamook, Oregon, to meet one of her old high school friends, Jack Vantress.

At first glance, Jack was a very intimidating man, especially to three young boys. His head was a solid brick framed with a mop of black hair and an unruly black beard. He'd fought it out in the jungles of Vietnam, and after many brutal battles he took a bullet through the hip. Through rehabilitation and exercise, he'd managed to recoup his strength, but he'd had a series of complicated operations, and surgeons had sawed a good four inches off his left leg. To compensate for this, he always wore one regular tennis shoe and one with an enormous heel, and he'd edge around sideways like he was seconds away from a shoot-out. When his dark eyes targeted you, it was easy to picture him scrambling up a mountainside, fighting off the Vietcong, grenades exploding around him. Jack was the kind of guy you just had to respect.

Back then, Abel, Dustin, and I weren't yet experts at covering the bruises and welts our father laid on our bodies. We weren't yet skilled at explaining how we'd just fallen down a flight of stairs or walked into a door. And even if we had been, Jack already knew about our daily hell. He was my mother's confidant, the person she turned to when she needed a shoulder to cry on, and although they were just friends, my father did everything he could to separate them. I think that of my mother's few friends, Jack was the one my father hated most of all. Jack was everything my father was not. A strong, loving man with a healthy family. A man who cared. My father's hatred for him ran so deep that years later, shortly after I defeated B. J. Penn in the Ultimate Fighting Championships, he called Jack's son and told him that I was the bastard child of Jack and Marlene. Even today, my father's delusions never fail to amaze me.

Anyway, I will always remember that day we went to Tillamook. I was pestering Jack to tell us what it was like to crawl through the jungle with a gun on his back, and he finally told me to quiet down because he had something important to tell us. I thought that maybe he'd describe what it was like to be tied to a bamboo rack, but instead he announced that he and my mother had decided that we three boys should get involved in sports. He thought we should become wrestlers, just like him.

"Wrestlers?" I thought. The word meant absolutely nothing to me. Although I had been secretly dreaming of my escape from the Backside, it never occurred to me that wrestling was the way to do it. The idea didn't exactly set off any bells and whistles in my head.

Then Jack said some more. After laying out for us what the sport entailed, he added that he was actually coaching a boy who was destined to become a champion wrestler. "Champion" was the word that did it for me. Champions weren't the kind of people who shoveled horse shit for a living or spent half their lives in jail. Champions were the kind of people who proved their fathers wrong.

Of course, my thoughts weren't quite so clear back then—hell, I was still wiping my nose with my wrist. I do remember, however, that I felt a kind of freedom as I listened to Jack talking about the sport. He had been involved in wrestling for more years than I could count, and he did his best to explain the sense of pride that comes with competition. And Jack also hinted that while wrestling couldn't fix everything that was wrong with our lives, it could, over time, help to heal the wounds.

After we got home from Oregon, one of the first things my mother did was enroll us in a wrestling program at Cedar River Elementary. It could have been Jack's influence on me, or it could simply have been that I was made to wrestle, but the first time I stepped onto the mats I knew that I'd found a special place, a place where even my father couldn't touch me. I don't think Jack could have guessed what wrestling would do for me and my brothers during that first year, or how far wrestling would take us from our father's domination, but to this day I love that man deeply for caring about three lost boys.

At last I had something besides fear to get my blood pumping. I did somersaults and cartwheels. I duckwalked. I roughhoused with other kids, which is something I rarely got to do while working long hours on the Backside. Looking back on my first experiences on the mat, all I can recall is joy. No one demanded that we be better than everyone else. No one instilled a thirst for conquest in us. We just got out there and went crazy. The closest I get to that sense of bliss nowadays is when I grapple with my teammates at Miletich Fighting Systems. Although we're some of the best hand-to-hand warriors on the planet, once we finish drilling our techniques, it's all about having fun.

Despite the casual approach taken in elementary-school wrestling practice, it quickly became evident that Dustin was a natural. He had balance; you couldn't take him down. Sometimes, he had two or three kids trying to blow him over, and after he toppled them one-by-one, he'd stand there with an odd smile on his face as if to ask, "Who's next?" He had the agility of a cat and the motor skills of a kid twice his age. It was amazing. When I was out there, I'd get punished and pushed around; when it was Dustin's turn, he wouldn't even break a sweat.

At the end of our first year of wrestling, there was a tournament for tike wrestlers in Oregon. Dustin won effortlessly. He had talent coming out of his ears, but wrestling didn't fit into the life he was trying to build. To this day, I believe that he'd have made it to the Olympics if he'd only stuck with it, but for Dustin, darker options were always more alluring.

I had to work harder to win my share of medals, and my mother was right there rooting for me. Even if she had worked a twelve-hour day, she'd make time to coach us on our moves when she got home. And she knew what she was doing. She'd sometimes go to tournaments we weren't competing in just to learn how things were done. Then she'd use that knowledge to make sure we were doing our moves right. "Your ass is sticking out too far," she would say. "You're not changing levels properly when you're shooting in." And when we were lazy, just moping around, she'd gather us together and make us drill our sprawls or work our takedowns.

My mother brought the family together—at least, the part of the family that mattered. As you might imagine, my father was angry that we were wrestling. If he caught sight of us practicing, he'd tell us that we were wasting our time. But my mother never let his abusiveness get to her—not as far as wrestling was concerned. She went on drilling and coaching us, hoping that wrestling would someday lead us to understand who we were.

In my case, that kind of understanding didn't come until junior high school. When I moved up to the seventh grade, living under my father's rule, and living on the Backside generally, started to get to me in a serious way. Each day, I grew more lethargic. But my wrestling coach, Russ Hayden, changed that situation fast. Unlike my elementary school coaches, Russ didn't let me goof off at practice. According to him, we were now in the big league. There was no time for somersaults or duckwalks. I had to start busting my balls every time I stepped into his gym.

He pushed me to my limit every afternoon, and as a result I grew more in the two years I spent under his tutelage than I have in any other two-year period since. By not letting me give up and turn my back, Russ taught me how to be a man.

One of the more important lessons he taught me was at a tournament I entered in the seventh grade. I was matched up with a kid I should have been able to beat in my sleep, but I was feeling lazy and tired, and I just didn't want to make the effort. I was losing on points, and all of a sudden Russ started shouting from the sidelines, "You're throwing it all away! You're not even wrestling! What the hell are you doing?"

Once I registered what he saying to me, I got angry and flipped the kid over onto his back, pinning him. When I approached Russ after the match, I thought he would be proud, but instead he turned away in disgust. I ran after him, proclaiming that I had won. I had thought that as long as I came out on top, I would earn his respect, but he was pissed because I hadn't given it my all right from the start.

"Winning doesn't matter," Russ told me later. "It's how you win that counts. It's the same with everything in life. The goal doesn't mean shit—what matters is the path you take to get to it."

Russ Hayden's lessons didn't end on the mat, either. The junior high was small, and he was a teacher as well as a coach. When I walked into his classroom for the first time, I was certain that I'd breeze through the work because we were on such friendly terms through wrestling. But the first time I messed up, he chewed my ass. I was practically speechless. All I could say was, "But I'm your best wrestler!"

"When you're in my classroom, you're not a wrestler, you're a student," he told me. "Now sit your ass down and get back to work."

So I got back to work. I was convinced that Russ hated me. But at our 3:00 p.m. practice, he was my best friend again. When I asked him why he'd been so harsh, all he said was, "There's a time and place for everything."

There was, indeed, and for the two years the Pulver boys were under Russ Hayden's instruction, there were glowing moments on the mats and at competitions. Wrestling became the escape route I had been searching for. As long as I kept winning, kept pleasing my coach, kept drawing cheers from the fans, I could forget about my father's ritualistic torture and send my mind to a place where I was king.

The thrill of victory never lasted long, however, and as I came down from the high of winning a big tournament I would once again find myself susceptible to my father's demeaning speeches and physical abuse.

Almost daily, I would bounce back and forth from being a winner to being a loser, and I began to realize that there were two people living inside of me. One cowered at the sight of my father; the other thrived on the encouragement of my mother, my coaches, and the fans. Those two people were constantly at war, and when I closed my eyes at night I could actually hear them arguing. One would say, "You're nothing but a loser. You might as well quit wrestling now." The other would come back with, "That's bullshit! You're a wrestler, destined to become a champion."

I didn't know which voice to listen to, so I just kept going. With each medal I brought home, I began to feel more confident, more sure of who I was. Unfortunately, the fact that I remained undefeated throughout my time at junior high meant that I didn't learn the reality of competition. When I got to high school, I finally learned that no one wins all the time, but by then my foundation had already been built upon victory.

At the first sign of stormy weather, I once again found myself treading water, trying to stay afloat.

4

Far Away

At high school, I found myself among the big boys. Everyone was larger than me, stronger than me, and to the champion wrestlers who got the crowds riled up at every Friday-night tournament, the sport was a way of life. They trained three hours a day, every day, and if one of them discovered he was a few pounds overweight, he'd do whatever it took, short of killing himself, to drop the excess weight.

Despite having a disadvantage as far as weight and experience went, I did well during my freshman year, but not great. After going undefeated for the previous two years, I felt that the losses I suffered were life-threatening. And they were. As I have already mentioned, winning was the way I stayed sane. Without victory, I was nothing. I was just an abused child who was destined to work on the Backside for the rest of his natural life.

Instead of sitting down and trying to think of some other way to cope with the insanity, a way that wasn't so utterly demanding and risky, I did the only other thing I could do. I got better. A lot better.

The biggest leaps and bounds that I made in my wrestling came the summer after my freshman year, when I was training at the Southend Boys and Girls Club in Tacoma. As one might suspect of a boys and girls club located in the heart of a ghetto, the place was a wreck. Outside was a weed-choked baseball field enclosed by a rickety fence, and inside there was just an old basketball court with a warped floor. There wasn't even a wrestling room—we'd simply pull the mats out on the hardwood floor and get down to it while other kids played Ping-Pong next to us. The thing that made the Southend so special—the thing that allowed me to harness the talent I was born with—was the coaches.

Dan and Randy Staab were their names, and to this day, when I picture them in my mind's eye, they resemble two gods sitting on Mount Olympus. If I had to name the Greek god Dan most resembled, it would be Hercules. The guy was almost as wide as he was tall, and he had a deep voice that commanded respect. Just like Jack Vantress, he had black hair and a black beard. And, just like Jack—with his one short leg—Dan had a minor physical abnormality: he was missing the tips of two fingers. Randy was Dan's antithesis. He was skinny, he always wore a dopey smile, and he had long, curly hair and a smoker's laugh.

Although they were brothers, and although they were both deeply committed to making a difference in the lives of a few boys, the Staabs approached wrestling in opposite ways. Dan was the hard guy, the guy who busted your balls if you didn't do what you were told, or if you tried to pussyfoot your way through practice. Randy was the good guy, the fun guy, the guy who was always laughing and trying to make us smile.

Together they made the perfect coaching team, and I don't say this lightly. Whatever they did and however they did it, they created the baddest, meanest group of young wrestlers in the state—arguably in the whole country. We were called the Torro Wrestling Club, and every boy who set foot on the mats, from sixth grade through high school, knew who we were. If a kid entered a tournament and saw that he would be competing against one of us, he shit a brick. We were that bad.

But Dan and Randy Staab didn't let us cruise along on our reputation. They saw to it that we busted our asses each and every day. Today, I can't imagine doing the kind of workouts I had to do back then, even though I'm the number-one lightweight mixed martial artist in the world. When we were getting ready to go to Gillette, Wyoming, to compete in the Western Regionals against wrestlers from thirteen other states, our coaches had us training for four hours a day. Our warm-ups alone would last an hour and a half. We'd run around the mats, drop down and do push-ups, then start running again, hour after hour. We'd do single-leg takedowns, one after the other, with no break in between, and then we'd get tossed into the pool to swim laps until we puked. They worked us like mules, but at the same time they treated us like we were worth all the gold in the world.

I felt a lot of love that summer. Just a few weeks before I was to start my sophomore year at school, Dan took me to Montana to compete in an AA wrestling meet. We took our time getting out there. I remember that we camped by the side of a river one night and shot off fireworks and fished. I lost one of my shoes in the current, and Dan gave me a pair of his own. We laughed together and ate by our campfire, and the whole time I couldn't help but wish that Dan was my father. The experience affirmed for me that not every father smacked his kids around. It gave me hope, plain and simple.

After we got to the meet, Dan continued to educate me. In my first match, I was pitted against a Canadian who was as strong as hell and moved like lightning. By the end of the first round, he was up thirteen points. I knew that if he got two more, he'd automatically win. Trailing so far behind, I was convinced that there was no way I could come back, so I crawled off the mat and went crying to Dan.

Looking me straight in the eyes, he demanded, "What the hell are you crying for? You going to give up?"

"He's killing me," I whimpered.

Dan slapped me across the face. "What's your problem, Jenny?"

"My name's not Jenny!"

"Well you're sure acting like a Jenny, Jens. I'm going to call you Jenny until the day you die if you don't go out there and push this shit."

So I went out there and pushed it, and I beat the Canadian kid fifteen to thirteen. Dan wouldn't let me quit. He'd give me all the love he had to offer, but he would not let me quit, and that made me feel like I was worth something. My wrestling coaches always treated me like a son, and I thank God for leading me to the right ones. That summer, wrestling gave me more than I'd ever dreamed, and it became the only thing I wanted to do.

When I strengthened my commitment to the sport, my mother did her best to help me. She drove Dustin, Abel, and me to wrestling tournaments over the continental United States. We went to Wyoming, South Dakota, Utah, and Idaho. She did it because she knew it was what we needed. It was obvious to her that I was nearing my breaking point, and if I broke, then the whole house of cards I'd so carefully constructed would collapse, and someone would end up dead. Guaranteed.

It was at these tournaments—far away from the fear that contaminated our days at home—that my mother's ultimate dream began to form. One of her fondest wishes while I was in high school was to have all three of her boys competing on the same high-school team. She dreamed of the day when I was a senior, Abel was a freshman, and Dustin was right between us. She imagined us, together, working a crowd of hundreds of wrestling fans into a frenzy, and the thought made her proud and happy. I think she could actually hear that crowd chanting "Pulver!"—as if the name could still be worth something after my father ran it into the mud.

But my mother's dream eluded her. As hard as she worked to keep us on the straight and narrow, Dustin was rapidly slipping away from her influence and moving towards my father's. Dustin still hadn't given up his goal of becoming a gangster, and he was getting closer and closer to attaining it. Not long after that summer had ended, Dustin dropped out of school and began a life of crime. And shortly after that, his mug appeared on the national television show *America's Most Wanted*. Dustin had always been Dustin, and he had his own idea of what it took to be a champion.

Then there was my father—the man who refused to relinquish his hold on his family for anyone or anything. By the end of that summer, he had practically destroyed our family's reputation at the racetracks. His drinking and his temper were out of control, and he'd become a threat to the safety of the horses. This situation, coupled with the fact that the rest of us were off doing something with our lives, enraged him even more.

It was during this time that I started praying even harder that wrestling would somehow save us all.

5

The Monster Upstairs

Night was the worst time at our house. With my parents' bedroom directly above mine, each time my father landed a fist I could feel the reverberations echo though my head. I can't recall how many times I woke up sweating in the darkness, listening to my mother screaming out my name, begging for me to help her.

Some nights, the stairs seemed a thousand miles long. I could hear my father huffing and thrashing, his paws slapping my mother's skin. I'd step slowly, trying to be as stealthy as possible, hoping to catch him off guard and wrap my arms around his neck before he had a chance to beat me back out the door. But most of the time he would hear me before I reached the top of the stairs, and he'd lunge into the hallway, a panting silhouette with arms flung open wide. Although he wasn't a large man, I swear that on those nights, when my heart was in my throat and my legs were like lead, he could have beaten the devil himself.

He'd stand there, daring me to take another step. Sometimes I would, and sometimes I wouldn't.

That's just how it was. I was the elder brother, and since the time I was in diapers I felt that it was my duty to protect my mother and my siblings. Although I don't remember it, my mother insists that when I was just five years old, I came to her rescue. My father had been at home all afternoon drinking with a bunch of his friends from the track, and without warning he decided that it was time to set my mother straight. He straddled her and began punching her in the face.

Not one of those men did anything! They just sat there, mildly amused, as if they were watching a horse race. When the situation became too much for me to take, I walked outside, picked up a rock almost as large as I was, and came back inside. "Get off my mommy!" I shouted, and I dropped the rock on my father's head.

We had some wars, all right, but I seldom walked away from the battleground feeling like a victor. It wouldn't have been so bad if I had been prepared for my father's attacks, but they were usually unexpected. He could be sitting there one minute, his mind wandering in some unknown land, his eyes glazed, and then suddenly he would come roaring back, tearing shit apart. When I was in junior high school, Dustin and I would sometimes get home early. If our mother's car wasn't parked in the driveway, we'd start fighting about who had to go inside first. Dustin and me tore into each other with everything we had, because we knew that if our father was in a bad mood, the one who stepped through that door first was going to get it much, much worse. Occasionally, when I'd find myself lying on the front lawn with a bloody nose and bruised knuckles, I'd try to get inside my father's twisted mind, try to get at what he was thinking, try to understand what kind of lessons he thought he could teach by beating on us. But the harder I tried, the less I understood.

The dinner table was one place I grew to fear. Many nights, there would be a heaping portion of brussels sprouts on my plate, even though my father knew that I was allergic to them. For a while, I'd spit them into a napkin and hide it under the table, but when that got too risky I started forcing them down.

Most of the time, I'd make it to the upstairs bathroom before throwing up, but on one occasion my stomach wasn't going to wait. Sitting in my chair, I vomited into my lap. The next thing I remember, I was five feet away from the table, my back slouched against the wall. When my vision cleared, I saw my father standing before me, his closed fist wet with my blood.

Over the years, I learned to take the punches, get up, dust myself off, and get on with my life. But the horsewhip terrified me. Some days, my father would carry it around as if it were his sword, just waiting for me to slip up. And when I did, he'd smile, take my pants down, and pull me across his knee.

A horsewhip is designed to train an animal with a thick hide, but my father hit me hard enough with that thing to lay welts on the backside of a horse. And he didn't stop with one or two lashes. Once he'd begun, he'd start frothing at the mouth and beat me until blood ran down the backs of my legs.

I don't recall how many times he did this to me, but I suppose a small part of me got used to it. Dustin sure did. Like all of us confused Pulver boys, he was thirsting for our father's love, but he alone was willing to take it in any way, shape, or form. When we had a babysitter, Dustin would raise hell, knowing damn well what the consequences would be when our father got home. Still, he'd do it anyway, and although he cried and screamed when it came time for his lashing, he seemed to relish the attention. Whatever lessons my father was trying to teach, Dustin took them to heart.

Abel, however, handled the abuse differently. While for Dustin abusive attention was better than no attention, for Abel it was intolerable. He burrowed deep down inside himself. At the track, he'd brush horses or shovel shit with a vacant expression on his face, and when all hell was breaking loose at home, he'd head for the nearest hiding place and read a book. He became an expert at hiding from our father, and, in hindsight, it seems to me that maybe his strategy was the best one of all.

But the worst thing was witnessing my father punching on my mother. I watched my body grow larger and stronger, waiting for the moment I would be able to fight back against the man who made our lives a nightmare. That moment finally came the year I was in the ninth grade. It was the day after Thanksgiving, and, after spending the holiday in Spokane, we were driving home in the van. I was passed out in back, exhausted from listening to my father rant and rave for two straight days, drunk out of his mind.

A large object came flying over me, jolting me awake. It took me a moment to realize that the object was Dustin. He hit the back door with a thud and crumpled into a heap on the floor. My father came crawling out of the passenger seat, his drunken eyes locked on Dustin, shouting, "You little cock sucker, I'm going to kill you!"

My mother was behind the wheel, driving the van down the freeway at sixty-five miles an hour, and the vehicle was rocking back and forth, throwing my father off balance. I guess Dustin seemed too far away for him to reach, because before I knew what was happening, he was hovering over me, his sweat dripping in my face and his hot breath stinking of alcohol.

Although I'd been asleep, in retreat from my father, he seemed suddenly convinced that I was responsible for everything—whatever had happened between him and Dustin, and all of his other problems in life besides. Staring into my eyes, he said, "If you say a fucking word, I'm going to fucking kill you!" I didn't open my mouth. I wasn't about to say a word. I just turned my face away. Then he punched me right in the teeth.

My world went black for a moment, just as it always did when he landed one of his better blows. When my vision started to clear, however, and I saw my father's fist rising again, something snapped inside me. For a moment, he didn't seem to tower over me. He was just like some kid I was facing fearlessly on the wrestling mats. For the few seconds that it took for me to squirm out from under him, get to my knees, and hook my arms around his legs, he was nothing more than an opponent.

The instant the first uppercut landed against my jaw, however, I knew that I had bitten off more than I could chew. Still, I refused to let go of his legs. Russ Hayden, Dan Staab—all the coaches I'd trained with over the years—had taught me never to abandon what I'd started, and, by God, I wasn't going to quit now.

Struggling to put my father onto his back and take away his leverage, I ate one uppercut after another. With every blow, my legs got weaker and weaker, until they felt like rubber. It was then that I realized that this was no competition, that we weren't trying to pin each other. This was a real fight, one that my father, lost inside his rage, was willing to take to the death.

I had come a million miles from the scared little boy who stood before the fireplace with the shotgun barrel in his mouth. Wrestling had given me a reason to live. Although I didn't realize it at the time, my life's path was already laid out before me, and it would one day lead me to become a world's champion. But at that moment, my father was trying with all his might to push me off that path. If I didn't do something to stop him, he was going to strike me until my brains came leaking out the sides of my head.

My mother's screams died away, and my vision narrowed until all I could see was my father's face. Before I knew it, I had released his legs and pounded him three times in the face with my left fist. I wanted to keep hitting him, but my arm froze in midair. Both of us were shocked, utterly dumbfounded. I was shocked because I had done the impossible: I'd punched a man whom I'd thought was invincible. My father was shocked because I had smashed the frail bones in his nose and bloodied his eyes. He understood that for the first time his kingdom was in jeopardy. His rule could be overthrown.

But the shock didn't last long. There was blood everywhere, and my father began spitting it in my face, swinging his fists wildly. He didn't land a single blow—not in the van, anyway. My mother, fearing for my life, swerved across three lanes of traffic to a rest stop so she could stop driving and help me. My father bounced around the van, his fists landing way off target.

By the time we came to a halt, it looked like an animal had been slaughtered in the back of the van. My father's blood had splattered onto the walls and ceiling. It was a pretty gruesome scene. Before any more blows were thrown, the entire family spilled out onto the blacktop.

While my father staggered in circles, trying to find his balance, Dustin behaved the only way he knew how and began popping off at the mouth, fueling my father's rage. Abel started crying. My little sister, Jamaica, started screaming. My dog began chewing on my father's leg. My mother walked around in a daze, watching her family come apart at the seams.

Then he came at me again. Although it was obvious

that he had the intent to kill, I didn't fight back. I just stood there trying to cover my face as he blasted me with jabs, hooks, uppercuts, and crosses. My mother leaped onto his back and tried to pull him off me, but it did no good. At that dismal rest stop somewhere between Tacoma and Spokane, my father was determined, for once, to finish something he'd started.

He beat on me for fifteen solid minutes. He gave me everything he could muster in his drunken state until he finally realized that I wasn't going down. That's when his fists dropped and he crawled back into the passenger's seat. Less than a minute later, he passed out from the alcohol and the blood loss.

By this point, my mother was a wreck. As we sped down the road looking for a gas station bathroom in which I could clean myself up, the blood that had pooled in my eyes dried and sealed my eyes shut. It was better that way, because I didn't have to witness the terror that aged my mother ten years that day. I wish that the blood had caked in my ears too, because then I wouldn't have had to listen to her cry and tell me how sorry she was a thousand times over.

Sometime during that ride, I said to her, "Fuck it. Don't worry about it. We'll make it through this." It wasn't until after I heard my own words that I knew I was right. My father had dished out his worst, and I was still alive. And I was getting bigger, harder, more callused. Pretty soon, I would be looking down on that pathetic little man, wondering why I had ever been so afraid of him.

6

Showdown

During the summer that I spent with the Staab brothers at the Southend Boys and Girls Club, my mother purchased a van with her own money and took us to meets across the United States. As I have already mentioned, we had a blast. Those trips introduced us to the world, and although I cherished every minute of them, there was a downside to being away from home for several days at a time.

When we returned from our little getaways, my father would usually be in a drunken stupor. Over the years, my mother had learned to read him, and she could usually predict his violent episodes. She knew when to run and when to get us out of the house. But the familiar signs weren't there that summer. My father would have unpredictable outbursts of horrendous cruelty. It got so bad that we awoke every morning wondering whether this would be the last day of our lives. I thought my father's aggression was triggered by the fact that we went away so much, slipping out from under his control, but we later learned that he'd become addicted to cocaine.

On our way back from Gillette, Wyoming, Dustin, Abel, and I sensed that if we returned to our father's house this time we wouldn't live to see the summer's end. Even though the idea of him hunting us down filled us with dread, the thought of returning to his domain was even more horrifying. In the van on the way home, we begged our mother to take us anywhere but back to that house. She looked into our pale, scared faces, and she came to a final decision. Our fear confirmed her own. Gripping the steering wheel tight, she declared, "Okay. We're going to leave him."

As it turned out, she had already started plotting our escape. She had considered taking us to her relatives in Oregon, and she'd secretly packed the things we needed in case she decided to go through with her plan. Now we were doing it. With every mile we put between us and our Maple Valley home, our resolve to leave my father for good grew stronger.

We made a few mistakes, however. The first was to stop in Spokane to visit some other relatives. We hadn't been there more than ten minutes when my father called. Now, I don't know whether he somehow intuited that we were leaving him or whether it was just coincidence, but the moment he heard my mother's voice he could tell what we were up to. He told her that he was going to Mount Rainier to blow his brains out. He'd pulled the old suicide ploy a least a dozen times since the day he headed into the backyard with his shotgun after removing it from my mouth. This time, though, my mother acted indifferent. She said, "Okay, but if you do it in the house instead, just make sure you don't leave a mess."

A few minutes later, we all hopped into the van and headed for the safety of Oregon. But at some point my mother's concern for her horses kicked in and she decided she had to stop at Long Acres to feed them. We pleaded with her not to do it, but she just couldn't stand the thought of her beloved animals going hungry because her abusive husband had finally decided to take his own life.

When we got to the stables, we were all on edge. As my mother fed the horses, I scanned the stalls, searching every shadow, expecting to see my father lunging at us with a pitchfork. But all I saw was hay blowing around my feet and flies buzzing above my head. As my mother was finishing up, I became convinced that we were actually going to escape.

I hurried everyone to the van. I wanted to be rolling down the freeway, lost in a stream of buses, cars, and trucks. But before we could climb in and burn rubber out of there my father came peeling up in the Suburban. Apparently, he'd forgotten all about killing himself.

Knowing what was coming, my mother tried to save us by swallowing her pride. "Hello, honey, how you doing?" she said in the sweetest tone she could manage.

We followed her lead, greeting our father as warmly as we could, but he wasn't buying it. With a furious glare, he looked us all up and down. Focusing in on the tank top my mother was wearing, he demanded to know whom she was sleeping with and started ranting about how he'd married a slut. Half of what he said didn't make any sense, and I could tell by the way he was shaking and grinding his teeth that he was high on some kind of speed.

Warning bells were going off in my mind, telling me to hold back, but the more he verbally abused my mother, the angrier I got. When I couldn't take it anymore, I stepped forward and said, "Dad, please leave her alone."

His bloodshot eyes snapped on me. "Shut up you little fucker, or I'll kill you!"

"No you won't," said Abel, coming to stand at my side. "And you leave my mother alone!"

It was the first time Abel had ever resisted his authority, and for a moment my father was stunned. Then he growled, "I'll kill every last one of you!" He started shuffling back and forth, trying to decide which one of us to maim first. In the end, he backed off. I'll never be sure if it was because he couldn't handle the fact that we were all covering each other's backs that day, or because beating his entire family to death just seemed like too much effort. For whatever reason, he didn't throw a single punch.

He did, however, do something that was much worse. Instead of tearing into us with his fists, which we'd grown accustomed to over the years, he hopped into my mother's van and drove off with her purse, our clothes, and all of our wrestling gear. In the blink of an eye, he robbed us of our only way to leave him.

That was the breaking point for my mother. She had endured years of torture, but that van meant more to her than her own physical well-being. She used the van to give us a break from the hell we lived in at home; she used it to express her love for us, to keep us alive as a family.

Hysterical, she fell to her knees. Never before had I seen her in such a miserable, hopeless state. It literally made me see red. I envisioned ripping my father's throat out. If I'd had access to a shotgun, there's no doubt in my mind that I would have hidden with it in the barn, waited for him, and then emptied it into his stomach.

But since my father was off doing God knows what with our stuff, I spent the hours of his absence consoling my mother. When I finally got her to calm down and pull herself together, she declared that we would leave as planned, but first we'd go back to the house to get some of our things. Once again we tried to talk her out of it, and once again we failed. She was determined to take a change of clothes, at least.

At the house, Dustin, Abel, and I were again scared out of our wits, and again our father showed up. He stormed into the house while we were packing and proclaimed, "I'm taking the van for good. I'm going upstairs to get my clothes, and then I'm taking the van forever."

If we could have believed him, we would have just let him go. But he'd been telling lies since before we could remember. We knew he'd take the van, sell it, get drunk, and then find us in a few weeks and beat on us some more. My mother's hysteria came flooding back, and she started clawing at his back and begging him not to take her van. My father, hoping for this reaction, laid into her with his fists, and then he opened his mouth and bit her, taking a chunk out of her arm.

My mother wasn't going to let him rob us, no matter how badly he hurt her. Bleeding, she followed him out to the van, pushed in front of him, and snatched the keys from the ignition. She had been milking cows and working with her hands all her life, and her grip was as strong as a man's. Once she got hold of those keys, she wasn't going to let go.

My father struggled with her for a moment, and when he couldn't break her grip he slammed her knee in the door. She fell backwards, still clutching the keys, and when my father came at her she tossed them to me. My father whirled around and rushed at me. I threw the keys over his head, back to my mother. Pathetic as it was, this was our only way to fight for what was ours.

After a few moments of this, my father had had enough. Instead of going for the keys, he simply went for my mother. He snatched her arm and wrenched it up behind her back. Then he smiled at me, knowing full well that I couldn't stand to watch her get hurt.

He'd learned a long time ago that by inflicting pain he could force us to comply.

This time, however, we weren't falling into our old patterns of compliance. I heard my mother screaming, pleading for me to help as she had a hundred times before, but I had no intention of handing over the keys. As my father struggled with my mother, I leaped behind him and punched him in the back of the head. He didn't go down, so I wrapped my arms around him, kicked his leg, and took him down, face first, onto the gravel.

Despite my prowess on the mat, I had some difficulty keeping him down. He kicked and hollered, throwing punches into the sides of my head. Eventually, he bucked me off, but when he scrambled back to his feet he found me standing there, ready to tear into him with my hands. Snatching up a log, he swung it at my head. The fight got so intense that we both were sure it would end with one of us going down—for good.

But it didn't work out that way. No victor was declared, because a few minutes into our climactic battle, the cops showed up. Abel, bless his heart, had called 911. He told them that his father was out in the driveway punching on his mother, and he was sick of us getting hurt all the time.

The Pulver secret had been exposed at last, and it took a ten-year-old boy to do it. The police came and took my father away that day, and I didn't see him again for a long, long time. None of us did.

7

Aftermath

I'd like to tell you that when my father was removed from our lives we became a tight-knit family and our house was filled with love. That's not what happened, however. Like any family that had only known fear, when we were released from it we had to go through a healing process. Sadly, people are sometimes too damaged to heal.

Dustin had already dropped out of wrestling, and instead of applying his talents in a positive manner he used them to sell drugs. He started hanging out at the racetrack more often, and sometimes he wouldn't come home for weeks on end. I didn't know where he went or what he did, but each time he returned to us he was a few thousand dollars richer. His outlook on life was becoming more and more cynical, and he was always wary of the law. I knew that it was only a matter of time before the Dustin I'd known as a child vanished completely, replaced by something as bitter and cold as our father.

As for me, I wasn't doing much better than Dustin was. Freedom wasn't the paradise I always thought it would be. Although I no longer had to worry about my next beating, I now had plenty of time to think about the things I'd seen and the lessons I'd learned. I tried to thrust myself into a normal life overnight, but I soon realized that I hadn't a clue what a normal life was.

A deep animosity towards authority blossomed inside me, and I rebelled against anyone who attempted to tell me what to do. I became uncontrollable in the classroom, shouting at my teachers if they gave me even the most trivial of orders, storming out when it suited me. In the months after my father left, I received many lectures from people who thought I could benefit from some parental advice, but their speeches only caused me to pull further away. Parenting was the last thing I wanted—after all, the man who was supposed to play that role had done little more than beat on me.

Every time I came up against a rule, I did everything I could to break it. A weight had been removed from my back when my father left, but it had been replaced with a chip on my shoulder. I began drinking heavily, skipping school, and fighting whenever the opportunity presented itself. Any kid who so much as looked at me sideways would get a punch in the mouth. I had stopped caring about life. My father had always said I was just a piece of shit, and I was trying hard to prove him right. I was heading down the same path as Dustin—except I still had wrestling. Wrestling was the one thing that kept me from dying in some ghetto or rotting in prison.

Despite my sophomore-year delinquencies, I always showed up for wrestling practice. Although I could sometimes still feel the alcohol swimming through my veins, clouding my thoughts, I pushed through it and gave 100 percent. It was during this time, when I was channeling all my hatred for the world into pinning my opponents to the mat, that I realized I still had two people living inside me.

The monstrous side of me, the side my father had created with his insane approach to the world, ruled the majority of my day, forcing me to act upon my every whim and do things that would later shame me. I could feel that side growing stronger and stronger, and every day I'd have to battle harder at practice to keep myself from walking out and giving up the only good thing I had left. Sometimes I would recall the lessons that my coaches had taught me over the years, or the trips my mother had taken me on, in order to maintain my focus. But despite all my efforts, the war raging inside me was soon burning out of control. My vision of the future grew so muddled that I couldn't see two days ahead. All I could see before me was the next hour, and all I could imagine was getting one over on the sons of bitches who had done me wrong.

At this rate, I was cruising for a meltdown before the year was up, but fortunately I had an eye-opening experience halfway though the wrestling season. Undefeated, I was the pride and joy of Tacoma High School.

At every meet, the stands were full, and as I looked up at the crowd I could see entire families waving banners bearing my name. The sight filled me with pride and a sense of purpose, and it also convinced me that no matter what I did outside the world of wrestling, I would always be worshiped inside it. Then, just before Christmas break, my coaches called me to their office and told me I was off the team because I was failing my English course.

I argued, of course. I told them that I was heading for the state championships. After spending all summer perfecting the skills I needed to climb to the top of the mountain, I had to be allowed to compete. But my coaches were unyielding. They knew me better than most, and they understood that I was teetering on a tightrope. They were aware that what they were doing was risky, but they were gambling that my drive to compete in the state championships would keep me from falling.

Even after being punched on all those years by my father, this was the hardest blow I had ever been dealt. I was at a crossroads: I could either join Dustin down at the track slinging drugs, or I could work my way back into the wrestling world. Although it seems like an easy decision—fall into a life of crime, or swallow a little pride and take control of my destiny—it was the hardest one I'd ever had to make. I couldn't imagine going back into my English class with my tail tucked between my legs and apologizing to the teacher, Ms. Bradley. I couldn't imagine sitting for hours in the library like a good little boy, catching up on my work. I wanted to say, "Fuck it all, I'm going down to the Backside, and I'm going to lose myself in a bottle."

In the days following my suspension, my dark half almost won the war once and for all. I vanished inside my despair. I didn't show up for school, and I avoided my coaches, my friends, and my family. I didn't want to be around anyone who would remind me of what I had lost. All I wanted was a bottle of liquor and a place to rest my head. But every day I stayed away, something strange happened. At 3:00 p.m., I would leap to my feet and stagger off towards school, aiming for the wrestling room. Halfway there, I'd remember that I'd been banished, eighty-sixed, kicked out, divorced.

Over the next few weeks, I'd sit on the sidelines during wrestling matches. It was as if I wanted to torture myself. Another kid—someone who didn't possess half my skill—had taken my place, and I watched as he grappled on the mats. I had to listen to the crowd cheer for him and wave banners stenciled with his name. I had to witness his defeats and then hear his opponents say to me, "You're lucky you're not wrestling, Jens, because the same would have happened to you!" All my hard work was circling down the drain.

More and more, I thought about my father—how he had pissed his entire career away and ruined our family name. Even though I hadn't the slightest clue where he'd gone or what he was doing there, I was certain that he wasn't up to anything good. He was probably wallowing in his misery more than ever, hoping that every ounce he drank would be the one to end his sorry existence.

I cried into my pillow every night, trying to stifle my screams. I ventured so far into the darkness of my mind that I found it impossible to eat, to sleep, to do anything but cry. And it was only after weeks of this milling around in the places where nasty things grow that I came to a startling revelation: being an abused child, no matter how tragic it was, was not a Get Out of Jail Free card. No one was going to feel sorry for me because of the things I'd gone through. No one was going to make my dreams come true for me. If I didn't do something, I was going to turn out just like my father, plain and simple.

So I went to see Ms. Bradley and told her that I was sorry. I said, "I'm sorry for being a dick, and I'm sorry for being an asshole." I told her that I wanted to work hard. To my surprise, she gave me a second chance.

I hit the books hard. I sat in the back of English class reading, agonizing over grammar, writing essays. After days of this, somewhere in that endless blur of words and sentences and paragraphs, I looked up and saw Ms. Bradley smiling at me. I smiled back. We had figured each other out, and I can't describe how warm that made me feel. Ms. Bradley was an elder, a person in a position of authority, and here she was smiling at me, even though I had called her every name in the book and stormed out of her class fifty times. Now she had made me feel like I was worth something, and that gave me hope.

In no time at all, I had brought my grade up to a C and was back on the mats. I had some serious ass-kicking to catch up on, and seeing that the season was almost over, I didn't have much time to do it. But there was no doubt in my mind that I was unstoppable, destined to win the state championships.

There was, however, one more obstacle for me to overcome first.

8

Nemesis

That obstacle was named Lenox Morris, and he was a
wrestler from Gig Harbor High School. Morris, like
me, was in the 135-pound weight division, and not
only was he a senior with over twice my experience,
but he was also an animal. For four years, he had been
chewing through his competitors, and this year he had
the state championships locked in his sights.

After my brief hiatus, I had continued my winning
streak. Although I had seen Lenox at several tournaments, we had never been paired up before, but I kept
an eye on him, because I knew he was the one kid who
posed a threat to me. Our first showdown occurred in
my last home match of the year. Both of us were
hungry; both of us felt unbeatable. I don't know whose
fans cheered loudest that day—all I know is that when
Lenox laid his paws on me, all of my power and prowess seemed microscopic compared to his. He tossed me
around like a doll, and then he shot in and scooped up
my legs. When it was all over and done with, I had lost
nine to one, and I'd suffered my first defeat of the year.

My resolve was shaken a bit by that defeat. I had sacrificed what I believed to be my pride in order to get back onto the mats, and now I couldn't produce the results I so badly desired. I had put everything I had into preparation, and when I went out there I had given it my all—but the other guy had still come out on top.

When I met up with Lenox again for the final match of the year, held the following week, I was pissed, scared, and determined. Apparently this was the right combination. This time, I didn't try to fight him off. Instead, I countered him with agility and balance. For the first two periods, neither of us scored a point, and the fans who filled the stands on both sides of the gym were going nuts.

At the beginning of the third period, I got the escape. Knowing I was up one point, I began to defend instead of attack. I was forgetting the lesson Russ Hayden had taught me. If I'd kept it in mind, I'd have realized that one point wasn't enough, and I'd have spilled out my heart until that final buzzer sounded, letting Lenox know who was king of the 135-pound mountain. But because I played it safe, because I was willing to scrape by with a narrow victory, I stopped wrestling. With only ten seconds left, he shot in, took me down, and won the match two to one.

So now I had another loss tarnishing my nearly flawless record. Another blow to my fragile ego. And, to top it all off, the morning after my defeat I open the local paper and saw Lenox's face staring back at me.

He had been nominated as Wrestler of the Year, and he was raving on and on about how he was going to crush me in the regionals and win the state championships. It was his time, he insisted, and Jens Pulver had to wait for his own. He said there was nothing Pulver could do about it—he, Lenox Morris, was number one.

Losing that match and seeing Lenox's remarks in the newspaper got me started on the first positive cycle of my life. I poured all of my energy into wrestling and left my father's world far behind. I vowed that when I met Lenox at the regionals, I would not quit or falter. If I let him beat me, I told myself, then I'd be letting people beat me the rest of my life. The time had come to shape my own future.

When I squared off against Lenox for the third time, the fans were on their feet. Everyone had his or her own perception of who was going to win, and as I warmed up on the sidelines before the match I could hear people debating: "Oh, look at Jens—he looks pissed"; "Yeah, but Lenox has already beaten him twice."

Now, I'm not going to give you a blow-by-blow account of our match. Just let me tell you that we went wild, attempting takedown after takedown. He pushed me so hard that by the end of the second period I was exhausted and wanted to throw in the towel. But I didn't. I came right back at him with power I didn't know I had, and with only a few seconds left on the clock, I took him down and won four to three.

Our battle for the state title a few weeks later went much the same way. Once again we gave it our all, and once again I came out on top. Lenox might have beaten me twice, but I had persevered. That's when I really started taking my wrestling coaches' lessons to heart; that's when I truly started believing that it's the path that counts, not the pot of gold. The state title meant little to me; it was my back-and-forth battle with Lenox that I cherished. I knew that from that moment on, every time I got knocked down, I would come back twice as hard.

I rode the high for an entire week. Everywhere I went, people knew my name and would come up and congratulate me. At last I felt like a true champion. Then, a few weeks later, when the news of my victory began to get old, I was blindsided by such a deep depression that I just wanted to die. One night, I cried like I had never cried before, and then suddenly I had my father's shotgun in my trembling hands.

"Jens! What are you doing?" screamed my mother. My wailing had woken her, and she stood in the doorway of my room, her hands to her face, looking like she was trying to tear herself out of a never-ending nightmare.

"I want to die so bad," I cried, "but I just can't do it."

"Why, baby? Why you want to do that?"

I opened my mouth to answer, but nothing came out. The truth of the matter was that I didn't know why I no longer wanted to live. I had won the state championships, and yet I felt so cold inside. That coldness was spreading throughout my entire being, and I no longer had the strength or the will to fight.

The next day, my mother took me to a psychologist. After many painful hours of talking, the shrink concluded that the reason I had been so determined to win the state championships was that I had to prove to my father and myself that I wasn't a loser. I had achieved my goal, but when the glow of victory had faded, I had seen that I was still Jens—a boy struggling to cope with his brutal childhood. No matter how great a wrestler I became, the past would haunt me forever.

Hearing my problem expressed in words gave me something to work on. It gave me something to overcome. But at the same time it showed me just what a long, hard battle I had ahead of me. And things on the home front were as dismal as ever.

My mother slaved, sometimes twelve hours a day, so that we could keep the house. The state helped us out with food stamps, but it embarrassed my mother so much to use them that she'd drive for hours to shop in markets where nobody knew her. At one point, she was thrown from a horse and her leg was shattered, requiring a dozen steel pins and a plaster cast. A week later, when the money stopped coming in, she broke the cast with a rock, pulled it off, put on a brace, and got right back to work. Providing for us was all she did. She didn't have a social life. She didn't have boyfriends. All she had were her kids, her work, and her unfading memories of years of abuse.

Seeing my mother reduced to such a state made me realize that if I was ever going to leave my past behind, I'd have to go away. But first I had to finish school, so over the next two years I knuckled down and brought up all of my grades. I broke away from the racetrack completely. I also grappled like crazy, challenged and motivated every day by fellow wrestler Ricky Christian.

I had known Ricky most of my life. His parents were horse groomers on the Backside, so, just like me, Ricky had grown up at the track. Another thing we shared was a troubled family life. His mother fought constantly against drug addiction, and his father was a recovering alcoholic. Although he never had to contend with abuse, Ricky was left to fend for himself as a youngster.

As children, Ricky and I had run with the rest of the Backside boys, as curious and mischievous as a pack of wildcats. One thing about Ricky, however, was that he always knew what he wanted—and it had nothing to do with horses. Despite their problems, Ricky's parents had been wise enough to steer him towards sports at an early age. He played baseball and football, but it was wrestling that captured his heart.

And Ricky had talent on the mats. Although he stood just under five and a half feet, when he got hold of you, you'd swear you were wrestling a giant. After all the turmoil of my sophomore year had passed and my head had started to clear, I recognized Ricky's talent and latched onto him at every practice. I had the idea that he was the one kid who would push me even if I was tired, lazy, or distracted. I was right. For two years, the two of us were practically inseparable, and we motivated each other continuously. In his senior year—he was a year ahead of me—Ricky went undefeated, took his third state title, and broke the school's takedown record. By the time he graduated, he had impressed dozens of college scouts and had plenty of top schools to choose from. He chose Boise State, in Idaho.

When Ricky went off to college, I was left behind at Tacoma High School to fend for myself. I came second in the state championships that year, and I believe Ricky's absence was the reason. I had no one to push me, no one to challenge me. Every day, I went to practice ready to train as hard as I had with Ricky, but no one wanted to grapple with me because I was giving beatings. No matter how hard I worked on my own, I couldn't get the kind of punishing workouts I'd had when Ricky and I were a duo.

My final season was a mediocre one, but by the time I graduated high school, I'd won two state wrestling titles and a national one. A number of recruiters had dropped by to see how well the eldest Pulver boy could wreck shop, and I received invitations from several colleges, including the University of Minnesota.

This, finally, was my ticket out of Seattle, but I wasn't as thrilled as I thought I would be. I was feeling overwhelmed. That summer, I drifted back to the Backside, and I broke horses in the heat. For the first time in my life, my future was wide open. When I closed my eyes, I could see a million different roads heading off to the horizon, and I hadn't a clue which one would take me where I needed to go.

Often during those long days of backbreaking work, I'd think about Ricky. I'd imagine him at a college tournament, hordes of fans chanting his name, and a smile would spread across my face. But I still didn't know if that path was for me. Strangely enough, after avoiding the Backside for such a long time, I once again found joy in waking up to the smell of horse shit. The gentle nature of the horses calmed me. I can't honestly say where I would have ended up if this tranquility hadn't been suddenly disrupted, making it clear to me that as long as I stayed on the Backside—or in the Seattle area—I would remain locked in the embrace of my past.

Just a few weeks before colleges across the nation started their fall semesters, I got word that Dustin had been arrested. He'd gone into a Seattle ghetto to make a drug deal; there, he was beaten and robbed in a stranger's apartment and then thrown out the door. Unable to withstand such a blow to his pride, he knocked on the apartment door a few minutes later. When his assailant answered, Dustin put two bullets in his chest.

With Dustin facing serious prison time, I again felt afraid for my future. If I stayed where I was, I could easily find myself joining my brother in prison a few short years down the road. So, spurred on by fear, I took action. The very afternoon I heard about Dustin,

I called Ricky in Boise to get his advice on what I should do.

"But everyone thought you were going to Minnesota," he said.

"No," I said. "I haven't signed anything yet."

"Don't go anywhere. Let me call you right back."

He called a few minutes later and told me to pack my bags and get my ass to Boise, because classes were starting in just two days. He told me that the school was going to pay for my books, knock off the out-of-state tuition fees, and provide me with whatever financial aid I needed. Ricky even said that I could live with him and his girlfriend until I got on my feet.

I didn't have to be asked twice. Ricky was my mentor, in a way—the person I looked to for guidance. Growing up on the Backside, where little kids were sucked in then spit out years later as directionless drug addicts and alcoholics, he'd built himself a mountain of dreams. If he thought that Boise State could accommodate his dreams, then it could sure as hell accommodate mine.

I set out for Boise two days later, and I thought I was leaving my father's shadow behind, but what I learned shortly thereafter was that your demons follow you wherever you go. In my case, literally.

Mother Marlene holds a young Jens.

The wrestling Pulver brothers: Abel, Jens, and Dustin.

A few of the trophies earned under the tutelage
of junior high school coach Russ Hayden.

Representing Tacoma High School.

On the podium following a first place finish
at the AA State Championships.

Fly-fishing with the G-Loomis rod.

Versus Alfonso Alcarez at UFC XXII.

Training at Pat Miletich's gym.

Dusty at home.

John Lewis recovers from the KO at UFC XXVIII.
Jens celebrates in the background.

Battling Caol Uno for the bantamweight title at UFC XXX.

Versus B.J. Penn at UFC XXXV.

Versus Penn.

"And the winner, by majority decision, and *still...*"

9

Out There

The moment I stepped off the bus in Boise, I knew I'd finally found my home. In the parts of Seattle I ran in, the reek of urine hung over every alley, winos hassled you wherever you went, and garbage rolled around in the streets. Boise was the exact opposite: a spotless Midwest town inhabited by the friendliest folks you could imagine. People actually stopped their cars to let you cross the street, and if you needed directions, someone would always be willing to offer you a few moments of their time. During my first casual conversation with someone I met on the street, I learned that the previous year Boise hadn't had a single homicide. Their biggest problem was bike theft.

I spent hours just wandering around that first day, and when I finally found my way onto Boise State's downtown campus, the amazements kept coming. I discovered a scenic river winding its way through a seemingly endless expanse of trees and brick buildings. I saw students bustling around with smiles on their faces. It was almost too much for me to take, so I sat down on a rock by the river and listened to the babbling water, absorbing the beauty and breathing in the fresh air. Boise was everything Seattle wasn't. It seemed like the perfect place to start my life anew.

During my first week there, Ricky and I went to a party, and we found ourselves telling story after story about life at the racetrack. We had people clutching their bellies, falling over with laughter. I told stories that just a few months before I wouldn't have shared with my closest friend, let alone a group of strangers. But there was something about being in such a beautiful place and facing a wide-open future that made me feel disconnected from the past. It was as though the stories I was telling weren't a part of my life.

By coming to Boise, I had left everything behind. Here, when people heard the Pulver name, they didn't associate it with a drunk-ass father, a teenager who'd put two bullets in a man's chest, or even a reckless young wrestler. All of that was gone, and I was starting out with a clean slate. Instead of changing my name, which I had been determined to do in high school, I was determined to resurrect it. I planned to accomplish this by becoming an all-American wrestler.

On my first day at wrestling practice, however, I became aware of the fact that this was a monumental ambition. The wrestling team met in the wrestling room at 6:00 a.m., and Coach Mike Young took us outside. He had us run up and down the nearly vertical incline of Table Mountain for more than an hour. When he finally let us stop, I was sent, huffing and puffing, to the weight room. In high school, we'd never lifted weights in wrestling practice—you just got out there and wrestled. But things were different here at Boise State. We had an intense weight training regime, and we stuck to it seven days a week. Coach Young told us that first day, "You're here to wrestle. You're also here to go to school, but you're going to spend most of your time in here with me, so you'd better get used to it."

My first turn on the mats was another eye-opener. No longer was I the fiercest, most ruthless 135-pound wrestler around. While I was wrecking shop to become a two-time state champion in Washington, the five other wrestlers in my weight division on the Boise State team were doing the same in their home states. During my last few years in high school, I had become a flash wrestler—someone who catches opponents in high-risk moves. But that wasn't working with these Boise kids. They came at me like freight trains, shooting in once, twice, three times in a row, chain wrestling until they blew me over.

After a few weeks of getting my ass handed to me, I came to the conclusion that I wasn't working hard enough, and I promised myself that I would do whatever it took to rise to the top again. That meant buckling down, at least in the wrestling room. Although I was having a blast living with Ricky and his girlfriend, I needed to find a place to live that didn't interfere with my efforts to establish a competitive outlook. I decided to move into an apartment with three of my teammates: Joey, Danny, and Jeff. (Joey Gilbert, as a matter of fact, took much the same path I did after his college wrestling years were over. He too became a champion mixed martial artist, and he graced the Octagon with his wrestling prowess shortly after I did.)

The four of us were on the warpath, concentrating on wrestling to the exclusion of everything else. That's why it didn't take us long to turn our basement apartment into a shambles. We had two cats, Whitesocks and Takedown, and they kept kicking each other's scat out of the litter box. Clothing was strewn everywhere, and dirty dishes were stacked a mile high. When Danny left food in his bedroom and the ants moved in, no one called an exterminator—instead, everyone started sleeping in my room.

We didn't care about the sorry state of our abode. We only cared about wrestling. Every day, we hit the mats and busted our asses. Determined to be the best wrestlers we could possibly be, we let the rest of our responsibilities slide completely—including our schoolwork. I would stay up until 3:00 a.m. and then sleep until practice time. I showed up for classes once or twice a week, but my mind was always somewhere else.

The truth of the matter was that I didn't enjoy sitting in classes and reading for hours at a time. I just saw it as something that took me away from wrestling; the time I put into studying was time that could better have been spent learning moves or building strength. Looking back, I can't understand how I could have thought that this was the road to success. Maybe it all boiled down to the issue of freedom. Now that I had my own refrigerator, no one could tell me what I could and couldn't eat. Now that I had my own apartment, no one could force me to go to class.

Apparently, my experience of getting kicked off the high-school wrestling team due to my failing English grade hadn't had a lasting impact. I was still deluding myself that if I put in my time on the mats, practiced hard, and kept improving, then everything else would fall into place. Reality hit when my first-semester grades came in. It was obvious that if I didn't shape up, they were going to ship me out.

Thankfully, our apartment flooded during Christmas break, forcing us to move out, and instead of finding a new place with Joey, Danny, and Jeff, I moved in with some football players I'd met who shared an apartment right across from the school. They were a little older, and they'd figured out how to balance their athletics with their schooling. I followed their example, and my grades slowly improved.

Things were coming together for me in Boise. I had a great coach, a huge group of friends, and my social life was nothing to complain about. After studying and practicing hard all week, my roommates and I would go to weekend parties—there were dozens happening every Friday and Saturday night. At these gatherings, I finally started to feel like a regular person. I could drink keg beer and laugh all night without once thinking about my past. I was having so much fun that I began to believe that my troubled years were behind me. Then my father reentered my life.

It's strange how the worst things happen when you least expect them to. One Friday night I was at a party, and just as things got rolling I noticed a big cowboy hat bobbing through the crowd. This was not an unusual sight—many Boise State students had been born and raised on farms—but for some reason it gave me a terrible sinking sensation in my gut. Unable to take my eyes off that hat, I set down my beer, walked away from the group of girls I'd been talking with, and pushed my way through the crowd.

With each step that I took, my fear grew, until once again I was a terrified little boy. Although all my instincts screamed at me to run and hide until the man wearing that hat was gone, some other force pushed me forward.

"Hi," I said, staring into my father's eyes. I couldn't believe that the word had come out of my mouth. I wanted to yell at him. I wanted to tell him what a lowlife good-for-nothing he was. I wanted to demand that he tell me what he was doing here, in my town, in my life, among my friends. But even more, I wanted to punch a hole right through his face. There was so much I wanted to do and say—I had drawn up a list on those nights I lay awake, my eyes refusing to close as my brain replayed the past. I had pictured this confrontation a hundred times, but now that my father was actually standing before me, all I could do was say "Hi."

My father did most of the talking. He had a new girlfriend, Tammy, and they had moved to Boise with the intention of finding work at the local racetrack. They were living on the other side of town in a trailer. Tammy had found work, but because my father had been banned from almost every racetrack in the country, he sat in the trailer all day. He just drank, watched television, and thought about how he could ruin his eldest son's life by putting on a cowboy hat and tracking him down at some fraternity party.

By the time I left that party, my entire body was numb. I tried telling myself that I hadn't seen him, that it had only been a bad dream, but I couldn't shake the terrible feeling that had taken hold of me. All I could do was pray that my father would disappear again.

He didn't, of course. In fact, I was soon seeing him everywhere I went. A six-pack in his hand and a joint behind his ear, he'd beg me to party with him. He found out where I lived, and he'd show up on my doorstep unannounced with a giant smile on his face. He buddied up with my friends, and before long they were telling me how lucky I was to have a father who liked to hang out and drink with me. The problem was, he was always hanging out, and he was always drinking. And the moment the two of us were alone, the facade would drop and the real man would appear.

At some point during that confusing time, I somehow convinced myself that because I was bigger and stronger I should give my father a second chance. After all, if he so much as touched me I could break him in half. But if I had truly been a man, I would have found the strength to say to him all of the things I needed to say. I would have been capable of turning my back on him without the slightest hesitation, without a trace of guilt. But on one level, I was still just a terrified child longing for a father's love. I was dying to know why he had hurt me so badly. I wanted answers. I wanted a reason to forgive him and love him.

The moment I decided not to turn my back on him, however, my father ruined me yet again, and the life I had grown to love in Boise was over. Now, I'm not blaming everything that happened on my father. I made the choice to allow him back into my life, just like I made the choice to stop attending classes, start drinking heavily, and get into fights at parties. And when I dropped out of school, it was my choice as well. But one thing I know for sure is that as soon as my father showed up, it suddenly seemed so easy to start living the life of a failure.

A few months into our renewed relationship, I finally realized what a horrible mistake I'd made. My father was at my apartment, drunk as hell, and he decided to call Dustin, who had just been released from prison. After a few minutes of small talk, my father began cutting me down, telling Dustin what an asshole and pussy I'd become. Lying on my bed and drinking my beer, he said that I thought my shit didn't stink and that I was too good for my dear old dad. As Dustin listened, he said that if I knew what was good for me, I would get down on my hands and knees and suck his dick.

When I heard this, my entire miserable childhood came rushing back to me. I couldn't believe that I had let my father into my house, into my life. How could I ever love this man who was lying on my bed telling me that the only thing I had left to do was suck his dick?

But I was born with my mother's heart, and I didn't beat him down. I just stood there smiling, trying to brush the whole thing off. When I finally got him out of my house, a few hours later, I decided he wasn't welcome anywhere near me anymore, and although I managed to avoid him in the months that followed, the weakness I felt for allowing him back into my world would haunt me for an entire year.

10

Awakening

After I pissed away my scholarship and dropped out of Boise State, I was lost. Most days, I'd wake up at around noon with a pounding headache, unable to remember where I had been the night before. Sometimes, my shirt would be splattered with blood, but often, no matter how hard I tried, I couldn't recall the fight. My nighttime excursions began to blur together in my mind until the dark hours seemed like one long, drunken bar brawl.

I survived by flipping patties at a downtown burger joint, but the job only added fuel to the fire. Every time a waitress barked out an order, I felt the anger swell up inside me. Every time I pictured my fellow wrestlers out there on the mats, the crowd rooting for them, I'd grit my teeth and dump more fries into the basket. By the time I got off work, all I wanted to do was drink and fight, fight and drink. I didn't have to hate someone to shatter his jaw or break his nose. Fighting was just fighting, I'd been raised on it, and now that I'd completely lost my bearings, it was the only way I had to express myself. I wanted to tear the whole world down.

I kept up this terrible routine month after month, until even my closest friends could hardly stand to be around me. They were all worried, waiting for that morning when the cops found me in an alley, my skull cracked open and an empty bottle by my side. But there was nothing they could do or say to make me change my self-destructive course. I was lost to them and to myself.

Then, as fate would have it, an angel appeared and saved me from certain destruction.

Her name was Kelly Martin. She was a gymnast from Chicago, where she'd attended an all-girl Catholic high school. Just over five feet tall, she had long blond hair and soulful blue eyes. She really did look like an angel, and when she's old and gray I suppose she still will. In my eyes, Kelly was the one person who could do no wrong.

At Boise State, the wrestlers hung out with the gymnasts, so I'd seen Kelly around. One day, I saw her hanging out with a few girls I'd known the previous year, when I was still in school, and I went over to introduce myself. The moment I heard her speak, I thought, "She's got to be the purest woman I have ever met." As it turned out, she didn't drink, she didn't smoke, and she had never been to bed with a boy.

After our first meeting, I found myself going to wrestling functions just to see her. It was the end of what would have been my sophomore year, and I was finally ready to admit to myself that there was more to life than flipping burgers and getting hammered. I wanted to be around Kelly all the time. I didn't want to steal her innocence; I wanted to protect it. It seemed miraculous to me that such a fragile girl had never been harmed, and I became like a bulldog guarding the last flower in a field of thistles.

Although Kelly was quiet and kept most of her thoughts to herself, I could tell that she had an inner strength that was similar to my mother's. Sometimes we would be around each other for days on end and hardly exchange a word, yet she would always have a smile on her face, even when she was performing the most menial tasks. There was something calming about her presence, and with every hour we spent together I found myself digging deeper into my mind, opening doors that led to my painful past. I drank from her tranquility as if from a well, and as a result I was finally able to look at myself in the mirror for the first time in over a year. The person I saw staring back at me, however, was no longer an eager young wrestler determined to become an all-American. He was a younger version of my father.

That summer, with Kelly by my side, I began to understand something of my father's plight. He had grown up in a family marked by insanity and violence. He had lived his early years in constant fear, always searching for a way to escape, and when he discovered that he could ride like the wind, being a jockey became the only thing he wanted to do. He had dreamed of the day he would pull ahead of the pack to the thunderous cheering of thousands of racing fans. My father strove for greatness to save himself from drowning in the misery of the past.

At sixteen years of age, he became a licensed jockey and left home. I imagine that during his first race he felt much the same way I felt the first time I stepped onto the mats at Boise State. He understood how monumental his goal was, but he refused to be intimidated. Instead, he channeled all of his energy into becoming number one. The victories piled up, he became one of the best jockeys in the business, but then he saw that no matter how many times he won or how many trophies he walked away with, his past would always be with him. He would continue to wake up screaming in the middle of the night.

Instead of confronting his madness, my father found another escape route—but this time it had nothing to do with horses. He met my mother, a beautiful woman with a heart of gold, and he romanticized their union. He imagined their life together—the little house with the white picket fence, the children running in the yard. Such a life could overpower the hell residing inside his skull. It could give him a shot at being normal.

The fantasy served its purpose for the first couple of years, but when his second child was born, the voices began whispering to him again. They told him that he was living a lie; underneath, he was still an abused little boy. By this time, my father was so good at running that he didn't dare do anything else. He turned to alcohol and then drugs, and before he knew it, he'd lost his career, the only thing that had ever truly mattered to him. He began to hate the world and everyone in it. He made his family sorry for reminding him of his failure, for being a part of his misery, and that's when he became the demon he'd been running from his entire life.

I can't recall how many times I broke down, clutching Kelly's hand to get me through the pain. Although I felt like I was being ripped in two, so many questions were being answered. While I was growing up, I had always wondered how a man with such talent could harbor so much bitterness. But now I understood that when you're born with talent, people expect you to triumph. And, even more importantly, you expect it yourself. This takes the glory out of victory, because in your mind you're already there. Then when you lose, the illusion is shattered and the bitterness sets in. What I learned that summer was that if you're born with talent, then you're already on top of the mountain. The only direction you can take from there is down.

That's the way my father probably felt at the height of his career—since he was destined to lose one day, then he might as well beat fate to the punch and start losing right away. So I had learned something from my old man after all. As I looked back on my time in Boise, I could see that my life had conformed to the pattern of my father's, only on a smaller scale. It was all too easy to imagine myself twenty years down the road, drunk and hateful, still using my talent to win scraps in bars. Perhaps I would have had a family, and perhaps I would have smacked my wife and kids around just like my father and his father had done.

I cried an ocean of tears as these revelations started to flow, but Kelly stayed with me and comforted me with her smile. She was the one who got me through those dark hours, even though she may not have realized it. Without saying a word, she allowed me to see where I had been and where I needed to go.

I was lying on the couch with her the day that I decided to finish what I'd started. If I was ever going to return to the mats at Boise State and receive a bachelor's degree, I would have to go back to Seattle, confront my past, and earn my way back. It was a terrible thought, because I loved living in Boise, the town of a thousand trees. I loved the friends I had made there. If only I could have just snapped my fingers and returned to that moment when I first arrived in town with a clean slate and the goal of becoming an all-American wrestler. If life was fair, I could talk to the dean, and he'd agree to overlook my grades. But life wasn't fair, and the scholarship I had earned by busting my ass for years on the high-school mats was gone.

The damage was done, and all the wishing in the world couldn't change that. But now, as I look back, I see that it was better this way. All the wrestling talent I possessed wasn't going to take me where I needed to go. I could have surrounded myself with fields of roses, and I would have only seen the weeds. I had to return home and conquer old demons before I could move on. It was finally time to stop running.

11

The Proving Ground

Before I left Boise, I stopped by the wrestling room to see Coach Mike Young. My reputation as a drunken scrapper had grown in the year since I'd left his team, and I could only imagine the stories he'd overheard in the locker room. But instead of turning away from me in disgust, Coach Young shook my hand.

"I'll be back," I told him. "I fucked up bad, but I swear to God I'll be back to finish what I started."

He studied my face for a moment. "I know you will, Jens," he said. "Go do what you need to do, and then come back here where you belong."

Later that day, I hopped into the '86 Nissan Sentra I had purchased with the last of my money and got onto the freeway. I could have headed to a junior college somewhere in Arizona or Utah, but it was this kind of impulse that had gotten me into trouble in the first place. Before I did anything else, I had to take a step backwards and conclude my childhood, and I had to go home to Washington to do it. Seattle, my hometown, had beaten me down and pinned me more times than I could count, but now I was going to hit back twice as hard and show that god-awful place that I was the meanest son of a bitch alive.

As I drove through the lifeless Nevada desert, my mind kept jumping ahead two years to the day I would graduate from Seattle's Highline Junior College. I'd head straight back to Boise, where I'd be welcomed by Kelly and my wrestling teammates. There would be a celebration, and later that night I'd sit with Kelly and both of us would be smiling.

My daydreams evaporated, however, the moment I arrived in Seattle. Walking through the grim and dirty downtown, lost among the hordes of city folk angrily bustling to and fro, a terrible weight came crashing down on my shoulders. My goal suddenly seemed so far off, and I knew without a doubt that the next two years would be among the hardest I'd experienced. I promised myself that no matter what happened, I wouldn't abandon my mission of returning to Boise. I was once again at war, and I had to adopt a combat mentality.

I didn't want to see old friends who had clung to bad habits. I didn't even want to see the people who'd made the most positive changes in my life, because they would certainly say things like, "You got to wrestle, you didn't have to pay a cent, and you pissed your chance away on alcohol and fighting?" If I saw them, I would have to tell them the truth. I would have to say, "Yes, I pissed it all away."

Because I didn't want people to know what a failure

I was, I made myself invisible. I moved into a dilapidated neighborhood called Sea-Tac, and almost every night there was a gang fight or a stabbing in front of my low-rent apartment complex. I told myself that living in an environment where I had to watch my back constantly would keep me on my toes, but when my apartment was broken into only a few days after I moved in, I found myself spinning into a depression, absorbing the chaotic energy of the neighborhood.

A week before my first semester at Highline was to start, I concluded that hiding in my apartment was the wrong approach to take. I needed to get out and have some fun once in a while. So I went to a neighborhood party, but only a few minutes after I arrived a guy burst in claiming that someone was slashing tires out in the street.

My apartment had been robbed, and now my car, the last thing of any value that I owned, was at risk of being vandalized. If that happened, I couldn't afford to pay for the repairs. I wouldn't be able to get to school and back, and I might find myself stuck in Seattle for an extra semester.

Praying that my tires had been overlooked, I went running down the street to where my car was parked. When I saw that the tires were still intact, I breathed a huge sigh of relief. As a matter of fact, I even started to feel a little lucky—my tires were the only ones on the entire block that hadn't been touched.

Just as I was thinking that my time in Seattle wasn't going to be so bad after all, a man appeared out of the shadows to my right. He was African American, he wore dark clothes, his eyes were bloodshot, and he was trembling. He shouted, "Yeah, I got you now, mother-fucker!" and I saw that he was holding a pistol. I dropped down so low that my ass was the highest thing in the air. Then I scuffled along the pavement on all fours, picking up speed before rising into a full sprint. Before I made it halfway down the block, however, I heard an awful boom and heard a bullet whistle past my head.

Panicking, I looked around for an escape route. I hadn't a clue why this was happening—maybe it was a case of mistaken identity, or maybe I'd somehow pissed the guy off. All I knew was that my aggressor had at least five more bullets in his gun, and if I continued to run in a straight line, one of them was bound to hit me.

Before he could get off a second shot, I spotted a sliding glass door that had been left open. It was just like in the movies—I cut a sharp turn and dove into a stranger's apartment. I leaped over a couch and a chair and flew out the back door. I hopped fence after fence, tearing though backyards until I was back at the party house. Inside, I fell into a chair and sat shaking and trying to catch my breath.

After I calmed down, I told a few people what had happened. Someone said that he'd seen the tire slasher get his ass handed to him by a white guy earlier that day in a fistfight. I guess that didn't sit well with the slasher, because after tending to his bruises and getting high on crack cocaine, he'd hit the streets with his gun, ready to shoot the first white guy he saw. It just so happened that the guy was me.

My mission to get back on my feet and return to Idaho had gotten off to a bad start, but I saw it as a test. God had given me everything I wanted, and I'd spit in his face. Now he was offering me a second chance, but he was going to make me work for it.

The shooting incident reminded me that I hadn't come back to Seattle to go to parties. It made me realize that I had to be hard-nosed about everything. Before I could return to pristine Boise, where I could lie on the riverbank and rest my weary head, I had to climb out of this septic tank they call Seattle.

School started, and in each of my classes I sat with a pen in my hand, giving my teacher my undivided attention. When I wasn't at wrestling practice, I was in the library. With every homework assignment I completed and with every test I aced, my enjoyment of the work I'd taken on increased. If school and wrestling had been the only things I had to tackle during those two years, the time would have passed as quickly and easily as a sunset. Recalling that period, I'm still amazed that with all the mayhem that was about to occur I managed to keep my head above water.

My most pressing problem at first was finding a way to earn a living while I studied and wrestled. I refused to even consider working on the Backside, so, seeking nighttime employment, I went downtown one day and dropped in at all kinds of business establishments. I was willing to do just about anything, but the only place that was hiring was a sleazy little nightclub called the End Zone. It was located on Pacific Highway, but everyone called it Crack Highway, because that's where people went to buy illegal drugs. I took the job and started slinging beer at night.

As you might imagine, the bar's clientele was not of the highest caliber. One night during my first week at the End Zone, I stepped outside to get a breath of fresh air and saw a guy sitting in his car with the engine idling. He wasn't moving, and after a few minutes I walked over to the driver's side window to ask if he needed help. That's when I saw that his shirt was soaked in blood. He had five bullets in his chest.

Inside the club, things weren't any better. Every Friday night, members of a biker gang came in to get drunk and shoot pool. As far as my boss was concerned, my job was simple: keep their mugs filled. And under no circumstances was I to evict one of these guys from the premises—not if I valued my life.

I didn't see what all the fuss was about. Mostly the bikers just sat around trading stories. Then one night, members of a rival biker gang came in and all hell broke loose. Chairs flew and pool cues became offensive weapons. My boss pulled me down behind the bar and ordered me not to lift my head until the fighting was over.

It was exhausting to work in a place like that, but every night after I knocked off—at 3:00 a.m.—I'd go for a run down Pacific Highway. I'd pass gangsters sitting on bus-stop benches, hookers on the prowl, and crackheads looking for easy targets to rob so they could get their next fix. Of course, this wasn't the ideal jogging route, but with my mornings taken up with my studies, my afternoons taken up with wrestling practice, and my evenings taken up with work, the only chance I had to run was on my way home from the End Zone. And, believe it or not, no one ever messed with me. I guess they thought I was some kind of lunatic, running down the street in the middle of the night, sweating my ass off. That suited me just fine. The less conflict in my life, the better.

Unfortunately, conflict became the theme of my two years in Seattle—after my brother Dustin came back into my life. While I was off pissing away my scholarship, Dustin was busy achieving his dream in a big way. He was now the biggest drug dealer in the Northwest, and he had the cars and the money and the guns to prove it.

12

Oh, Brother

Dustin just showed up at my door one afternoon. He wanted to know how his long-lost brother was making out. Talking like a thug in a gangster flick, he rolled into my apartment wearing a black leather jacket, his hat twisted sideways.

Still, I hugged him with all my might. Seeing him after all this time brought back memories of those blistering-hot summer days at Long Acres when we'd sneak through the barns looking for mischief. I missed hearing about his exploits and spending afternoons with him on the mats. Although I regretted that we'd never wrecked shop together at high-school or college wrestling tournaments, I knew that it wasn't his fault. He'd chosen a different path for his own reasons. I'd escaped by going to Boise, and Dustin had escaped by embarking on a life of crime.

That night, we recalled old times; we talked about the Backside and all the pranks we had pulled. We shared stories for hours, and sometime in the early morning, when I told him I had to get to bed, he asked

me if he could stay. Something about his tone of voice
sent a shiver down my spine, but I said yes. Maybe he
had nowhere else to go, or maybe he just felt safe
being with his big brother—I didn't know. The only
thing I knew for sure was that he needed me.

Dustin showed up more and more often as the
months passed, and it wasn't long before he started
bringing his gangster friends with him. They took to
counting the day's take on my coffee table, and it was
sometimes as much as seven thousand dollars. More
than once, they invited me to join them in their she-
nanigans, but I was never tempted, even when I didn't
have enough money to pay the power bill. I turned
them down flat every time, but in the process I earned
their respect. They couldn't believe that I was willing
to endure instant-noodle-soup meals and long hours
at the End Zone just to get back to Boise.

I couldn't blame them. After all, they had never
seen the river that ran through the Boise State campus, or felt what it was like to wrestle in front of cheering fans, or be with a girl who made you feel special
without saying a word. All they knew were the streets,
living life from day to day, and cooking crack cocaine.

But the fact that some of his friends had begun to
look up to me became a source of conflict between
Dustin and me. Each of us was trying to win the other
over to his way of life, and if his friends admired me,
then he was losing that contest. Once in awhile, I'd
take Dustin to my wrestling meets, and when I'd look
up into the stands and see him smiling, I could tell that

he was thinking about all he had lost over the years. Perhaps he was even wondering how he could get it back. But the following day he'd be back out on the streets making piles of cash. He would flaunt his money and tell me how rich I could be if I would only join him.

Each of us finally realized that the other could not be swayed, and that's when the real problems began. The cops started coming around and asking me questions about my brother. They were sure I was involved in his dealings, and they hassled me every chance they got, sometimes parking for hours in front of my apartment. They couldn't understand how a poor kid living in Seattle's worst neighborhood could resist the temptation of crime, especially when that kid hung out with people who had pretty much given up on society. They found it impossible to believe that although everyone I was associated with was doing things their own way, I could still do things the right way.

But being confronted with the cops on a daily basis wasn't the worst thing I had to deal with as a result of my association with Dustin. One evening after practice, I was walking through my apartment complex when a young man stepped out from behind a tree and pointed a gun at my face. Just as he was about to pull the trigger, he realized that I wasn't who he thought I was—I wasn't Dustin.

Having my life nearly stolen from me only made me work harder to finish junior college, but every time I managed to take a step forward, Dustin pushed me back. At one point, he didn't come to see me for over a week, and I was worried about him. I knew that he was probably in jail, but I kept picturing him getting shot or stabbed and lying alone in a hospital bed. I tried telling myself that he had to deal with his own troubles, but that kind of thinking didn't help me sleep at night. Finally, I ran into one of his gangster friends and found out from him that Dustin had gone to Yakima the week before.

The first thing I did was call the Yakima jail to ask if they had a Dustin Pulver in custody. "Funny you should ask that," said the guy who answered the phone. "We don't have a Dustin Pulver, but we do have a Jens Pulver."

"No kidding," I said. "What did old Jens do this time?"

"He was carrying eighteen thousand dollars in un-explained cash, he was in possession of a stolen car, he was driving without a license, and speeding, and there's a weapons charge . . ."

The guy went on and on. When he was finally finished, I asked him what they were planning to do with "Jens." "Well," he replied, "we're getting ready to release him."

"Have you taken his fingerprints?"

"Yeah."

"But have you looked at them?"

"No. I think we just filed them away."

"Well, guess what?" I said through clenched teeth.

"I'm Jens fucking Pulver, and I'm sitting on my couch here in Seattle talking to you!"

Now the guy sounded alarmed. "Then who do we have?"

"Do your fucking job," I said, slamming down the receiver.

Ten minutes later, still in a rage, I called the Washington State Police and discovered that Dustin had been using my name for the last six months. Although he didn't have a driver's license, he had a twenty-thousand-dollar car, and every time the police stopped him he would give them my name and birthdate. And they had stopped him a lot. I had thirteen failures to appear, and there were thirteen warrants out for my arrest in the state of Washington alone.

Over the course of the next few months, I missed countless classes and wrestling practices as I went from court to court trying to clear my record. I called all sorts of government officials who assured me that my name was now red flagged in the police computers and that anyone claiming to be Jens Pulver would have to show identification. Despite their promises, every time I got two warrants erased, two more would appear. Dustin just kept racking them up throughout the western states.

Pretty soon, I gave up, because it was like running uphill with rocks on my back. And I couldn't afford the time it was taking. Clearing my name was not my most important goal, and I wasn't going to let my brother fuck up my future plans. I loved him, yes, but he was no longer the boy I'd grown up with. On those nights the two of us spent reminiscing, he might have seemed like the same old Dustin, but that side of him was coming out less and less often. I knew that if I didn't get away from him soon, I'd once again be heading down the wrong path.

We had it out one night in my apartment, releasing all of our pent-up anger. I learned that Dustin was ashamed of our mother—ashamed of the side of the family that walked the straight and narrow. He actually had the nerve to put down my mother's father, a man who had been awarded a Purple Heart during World War II for fighting the Germans for two whole days after one of his legs had been blown off.

"You think you're too good for everyone," he told me.

"Why? Because I don't sell drugs? Because I refuse to take the chicken-shit way out?"

"No. Because you're scared and weak."

"Jesus Christ," I said. "Listen to yourself. You sound just like Dad. You better take a look at yourself."

We continued to argue, and after about fifteen minutes, when things were really heated, Dustin pulled out his gun and pointed it at my chest. At that moment, I didn't care if he shot me. I slapped him upside the head and told him to get out of my house. He didn't argue, and the next time I saw him was on television. His face was being broadcast on the show *America's Most Wanted*, and in the back of my mind I knew that this was an accomplishment that Dustin was probably proud of.

This battle with Dustin took its toll on me, and once again I found myself trying to make it through the day without exploding. I tried to think of Kelly and all my friends in Boise, five hundred miles away, but my memories of my adopted home were growing distant.

A positive outlet for my aggression—something other than fistfights—was what I needed, so I went searching for one, and I met a guy named Alfredo, who was a purple belt in Gracie jiu-jitsu, a Brazilian martial art. I thought I might throw him around a little, maybe work out some of my frustrations, but once we began to roll on the mat, I found myself gasping for air. He caught me in choke holds, leg locks, and arm bars. It was a humbling experience, to say the least, but instead of losing my cool, I asked Alfredo to show me what he knew.

It was great. He taught me all the moves that weren't permitted in wrestling. I practiced with him every free moment I had, and although I didn't train with the intensity that I would later on, our sessions became my outlet. Occasionally, I would even participate in a challenge match on the wrestling mat. I'd go wild, trading blows with any opponent who was up for it.

Now that I had this positive activity to focus on, I felt like I was getting things back under control. During my second year at Highline, I had the highest grade point average of any 142-pound junior-college wrestler in the country, and, even more importantly, I became a national champion again.

But I had come back to Seattle to conquer my demons, and living half an hour from home, I hadn't really done that. Fortunately, my father forced me to. One afternoon just before I graduated from Highline, he showed up at my apartment out of the blue. Apparently, he no longer had a reason to live in Boise since I wasn't there, so he'd followed me back to Seattle.

"I'm hungry," were the first words out of his mouth. "Let me borrow your car so I can go get some food."

I didn't know what to think, and once again there were a million things I wanted to say but couldn't. All I could do was stand there and replay his words in my mind: "Let me borrow your car so I can go get some food."

Before I could form the word "No," he started carrying on about how he was starving and needed to pick up a check so he could buy himself something to eat. The more he said, the clearer it became to me that I could no longer stand the sound of his voice. I was late for wrestling practice, and the longer I listened to the words that were coming out of his mouth, the more I wanted to give him my car just so he would go away. Against my better judgment, I handed him the keys.

Because I hadn't taken Dustin up on his offer to sling drugs—and I was still working down at the End Zone for minimum wage—my car was the only thing of value that I owned. Despite the fact that I could no longer drive long distances for fear of being arrested on one of Dustin's warrants, it was still my most cherished possession.

As my father climbed into the driver's seat, I managed to call out, "If it isn't parked at the curb when I get home from practice, I'm coming looking for you!" He didn't turn around, and as I watched him drive off I knew in my heart that I'd made a huge mistake. When I returned home from practice that evening and my Nissan Sentra wasn't parked out front, I slapped myself in the face for being so stupid.

Twenty-four hours passed. Everyone I knew was calling me a fucking idiot. I tried to convince myself that my father was lost, or that something important had come up, but after another twenty-four hours, I had to face the reality that he had stolen my car. After three days had passed, I went looking for him.

I did a little research and found out where my father was staying. I got to his apartment complex, only to find that he wasn't home, but I bribed the security guard to call me the minute he got back. Then I went home and waited, letting my anger brew. I thought about all the pain that man had caused me. In my mind, I kept replaying what he'd said to Dustin about how I should get down on my knees and suck his dick. As the hours went by, I imagined more and more elaborate ways to hurt him back.

The next day, the security guard called to tip me off. I was too irate to formulate a game plan, so I just hopped on a bus and headed over to the apartment. His door was open when I got there, and he was sitting on the couch watching television. Too angry to talk, I held out my hand, hoping, for his sake, that he would make this easy. When he tried to talk, I told him to shut the fuck up.

"I'm just so mad right now," I said, "that I could beat you within an inch of your miserable life."

"You've got it all wrong," he said. "I was just getting it fixed."

"The car was never fucking broken!" I shouted. I was about to step forward, but then I stopped myself. If I took that step, it would turn into ten, and then I would be on top of that monster, beating on him with everything I had. I could feel the rage boiling up inside me, and I knew that once it started to boil over, I wouldn't be able to stop it. I'd deliver ten punches for every one he had dropped on my mother and me over the years, and by the time I finished there would be nothing left of him. I would be doing him a favor, but in the long run I would suffer. I had to think of my dream, about getting back to Boise. I couldn't do anything to risk losing what I had worked so hard for.

"I'm not going to hurt you like I want to," I said, "but as far as I'm concerned, you're no longer my father. I want you out of my life, and if you ever try to follow me again I'm going to kill you. Do you understand me? I'm going to fucking kill you!" Staring into my bloodshot eyes and trembling face, he understood perfectly.

When I got home, I was exhausted. It felt as though I'd just competed in the biggest tournament of my life, and I flopped down onto the couch. In a strange, distant way, I felt triumphant, but a few minutes later tears were streaming down my face. I had expelled from my life the man who had helped to bring me into this world, and although it was something I had to do, it pained me in a way I can't describe.

Shortly after that, I graduated from Highline Junior College. After the ceremony, on a Friday evening, my mother threw a little party for me at her house. There was drinking and dancing, and when the party was winding down, she presented me with a graduation gift: a handmade G-Loomis fly-fishing rod.

My mother showed me where she was going to have my name engraved on the graphite rod, and I stood there for the longest time, holding the thing in my hands and wondering why in hell she'd chosen such a present. My father had never taken me fishing, and I didn't know the first thing about the sport. Although as a child I had dreamed about standing waist deep in a creek and casting a line through the air, sometime during the last decade I had lost the urge. Now here I was, holding my first rod, and it just seemed like a very expensive pole with a string attached to it.

"Mom, you can't afford this. You didn't have to do this."

"I needed to," she said. Then I looked into her eyes and understood what the fishing rod symbolized for her. It was her way of saying goodbye. She knew that I had achieved all I could in Seattle, and that I would be coming home less and less often in the years to come. The rod was a way of telling me that she understood, and of sending me off in the right direction.

Then my mother told me that she was going to take me to Spokane the following week, and she added that I should bring along the rod.

"It'll be just like old times—you and me on the open road. You're all grown up now, and I don't know when we might get another chance."

"You're going to teach me how to fly-fish?"

"No. But I have a friend who would very much like to."

For the previous two years, while I was sweating it out in Sea-Tac, my mother had been rebuilding her life. She had a boyfriend, Guy, who was nothing like my father. He was a kind man with a good heart, and he treated my mother like a lady. Guy also happened to be an expert fly-fisherman. He had a ranch on the outskirts of Spokane, and we camped out on his land for an entire week.

Feeling the morning sun on my face as the breeze ruffled my hair reminded me of what I had been missing while living in the city. For hours on end, I stood beside the lake watching bugs skim across the water's surface. With no cops, gangsters, or drug dealers to distract me, I experienced utter tranquility—something I hadn't experienced since I left Kelly's side.

Even before I cast my first fly, I knew that I'd be a fisherman for the rest of my life.

By the time my vacation was over, all I could think about was returning to Boise. The man upstairs must have been listening to my prayers, because my official letter of readmission to Boise State was waiting for me when I got back to Seattle. I packed my bags and went to bed, but before I could burn rubber out of town the following morning, I was given a painful reminder of where I might end up if I screwed up this golden opportunity.

Shortly after midnight, I was awakened by a terrible scream out in the street. I tried to ignore it, to shut it out, but once I'd registered that it belonged to a woman, I rubbed the sleep from my eyes and staggered into the living room. Peering out the window at the street below, I saw a guy who was clearly high on crack cocaine holding a knife to a woman's throat. Surrounding them were twelve members of the Seattle SWAT team, guns drawn.

Before I could duck down to avoid stray bullets, I heard my bedroom window shatter. Keeping low, I ran to the bedroom, and there I saw a brick lying on my bed. Not sure what was going on, I carefully stepped over the broken glass, crept to the window, and looked down into the back alley. There I saw a gaggle of cops trying to break up a Mexican gang fight.

With a SWAT team out front and a riot out back, I sat on the kitchen floor, my head well below window level, and laughed until my stomach hurt. For two years, I'd lived among the worst of the worst. I'd been to hell and back to achieve my dream. And I'd done it in a way my father would never have been capable of. Not only did I find that immensely gratifying, but for some strange reason I also found it immensely funny.

I slept that night on the linoleum floor, but in my dreams I was already five hundred miles away.

13

A New Direction

Back when I was fifteen years old, I brought home a videotape of the first Ultimate Fighting Championships and asked my mother to sit down and watch it with me. At the end, just as Royce Gracie was hefting an oversized check for $50,000 above his head, I pointed to the belt he wore and told my mother that one day it would be mine. A doubtful look came over her face, and I could tell she was probably thinking, "You weigh 150 pounds, Jens, and you're going to win that belt? Keep shooting high, son."

Nine years later, I still wanted that belt, and when I got back to Boise I set out to get it. It's not that I'd stopped wanting to be an all-American wrestler; the problem was that an injury I'd sustained during practice was holding me back. While I was grappling with teammate Jesse Young, I broke a fall by planting my hands on the mat, fracturing both wrists.

Sitting on the sidelines for most of the season didn't affect me as it would have a couple of years before. I no longer measured my sense of self-worth against my achievements on the mat. I realized that there were plenty of other things that I was good at and from which I derived just as much satisfaction. Kelly and I had reconnected, and almost every weekend we escaped to the mountains and went fishing. I spent quality time with my friends, hiking, golfing, and mountain-bike riding. I also enjoyed school, because I'd finally found a direction that suited me. After two years of living in a ghetto, I decided that I wanted to major in criminal justice. When I graduated, I planned to work with troubled youths.

Between my studies and my social life, my schedule was pretty hectic, but I still longed for the thrill of competition. As soon as my wrists healed, I hit the wrestling mats. The competition season was almost over, however, so I shifted my focus to mixed martial arts. I was going to train for six months and then see how I fared in full-out hand-to-hand combat.

My wrestling teammates helped me any way they could. They hung a punching bag in one corner of the wrestling room, and whenever I needed to practice my submissions, one would willingly serve as my dummy. For hours every day, I trained myself to strike with my fists, knees, and elbows, and I perfected the few submissions I'd learned from Alfredo back in Seattle. Although I wanted to take my skills to the next level by training at an official mixed martial arts academy, after a thorough search I learned that no one in Boise taught reality fighting, let alone jiu-jitsu.

My options were limited, so I had to make the best of the situation. After just a few months of training in the wrestling room, I began entering underground cage-fighting tournaments, in which fighters were locked into a cage together for the duration of the bout. These underground events were held in back-yards, basements, and high-school gyms. Most of the competitions didn't even have a name, and none of them were sanctioned by the Idaho State Athletic Commission. I'd receive a call, and then an hour or two later I'd be fighting somewhere in the city for a novice promoter who hoped to make a few bucks by drawing a bloodthirsty crowd.

The events had the same rules as the first UFC: no biting, no eye gouging, no strikes to the groin. How-ever, these rules were rarely enforced. Competitors were usually street fighters or bar brawlers, and their only goal was to take someone's head off. Their skills may not have been top-notch, but their willingness to scrap made for some decent fights.

Because of my wrestling prowess, I dominated from the start. When a competitor came at me with his fists swinging, I'd shoot underneath him and take him down at the knees. Once he was floundering on his back and unable to strike, it was only a matter of time before I choked him out or caught a dangling limb and cracked on it until he pounded his hand in submission. In my first five or six tournaments, I rarely threw a strike. I stuck to what I knew, and I was able to defeat opponents nearly twice my size.

But these victories were minor ones. If I was ever going to rise in the world of mixed martial arts and fight in the UFC, I'd have to find a way to learn more. Wrestling was a powerful discipline, but everyone in the UFC knew how to wrestle. They also knew how to escape rudimentary submissions and land knockout blows while lying on their backs. It was one thing to dominate local underground fights, but dominating in the UFC was something entirely different. In order to do that, I would have to become a universal fighter.

I put the word out around town that I was looking to train with anyone who could improve my skills. Soon, all kinds of testosterone-laden tough guys were coming to the wrestling room to fight me. My fellow wrestlers protected me, turning away anyone who had alcohol on his breath. Occasionally I'd get to roll around with someone who actually knew a submission or two, but I still wasn't getting the training that I needed.

Growing frustrated, I decided that experience was the best teacher. Only a few weeks before school finished, I entered the largest tournament I'd ever participated in. It was an underground event, and it was held in a local gym, but it was well promoted and it drew a large crowd and a high caliber of fighters. I was supposed to be matched with an opponent who was only a few pounds heavier than me, but when he failed to show up, the promoter said, "I'm sorry I have to do this to you, Jens, but if you want to fight it'll have to be against a guy who's a lot larger than you."

"How much larger?"

"He's 210 pounds. But he's a boxer, so I don't think you'll have any trouble with him."

My years on the wrestling mats had taught me that if you battled a guy carrying a few—nevermind fifty—more pounds than you were, then you were putting yourself at a serious disadvantage. But I had come to this tournament to fight, and I wasn't about to turn down an opportunity to get more experience under my belt. "I'll do it," I said.

Twenty minutes later, I was locked into the cage with a guy who towered over me. As always, I stuck to what I knew. I took him down to the mat and beat him senseless with short, choppy strikes—it was all over in less than two minutes. I changed into my street clothes, packed my stuff, and headed for the door, but before I got there, a guy wearing a Gracie jiu-jitsu T-shirt stopped me. He introduced himself as Lowell Anderson, and he said that he might be able to help me with my fighting career.

Lowell had a jiu-jitsu academy ninety miles north of Boise, and after seeing what I could do to a 210-pound pugilist, he wanted me on his team. The following week, I made the two-hour drive to his academy. After I'd trained for only a few hours, Lowell pulled me aside and pointed to a poster on the wall advertising the Bas Rutten Invitational in Littleton, Colorado.

I looked at it for a moment, but I couldn't figure out what he was trying to tell me, so I said, "What about it?"

"We're going to enter you in that event," Lowell said.

"But it's in one month. Between school and work, I don't have much free time, so I don't know how often I can come up here to train." Looking at the poster again, I knew that the invitational would be nothing like the cage-fight tournaments I'd been competing in. If that poster had found its way into Lowell's tiny gym in the heart of Idaho, it had most certainly made it onto the wall of every mixed martial arts gym in the country. It would likely attract some of the best young hand-to-hand fighters in the United States—perhaps the world. Doubtful of my ability to compete with Japanese and Brazilian fighters who had been training for cage matches since they were old enough to walk, I said, "I don't think I'll be ready."

"You already are," replied Lowell. "Besides, John Perretti, the UFC matchmaker, is going to be in attendance. If you really want to fight in the UFC one day, this is your chance to make an impression."

Once I heard that, I put my apprehension aside and agreed to compete. I knew that I could go out there and get my ass handed to me within fifteen seconds, but I was convinced that if I didn't lay it all on the line now, then I wouldn't be any better than those black belts who brag that they're the best in the world without ever proving it. If I wanted to talk the talk, I had to walk the walk.

I made it up to Lowell's academy only two more times before the Bas Rutten Invitational. For his own reasons, Lowell chose not to show me the submissions I badly needed to learn, but this didn't shake my resolve to compete. If I turned down this opportunity, I could live to regret it, and after spending two years in exile from the town I loved, regret was a feeling I tried hard to avoid.

Arriving in Littleton, Lowell and I made our way to the venue, and I paid the fifty-dollar entry fee. My situation looked bleaker than ever when we discovered that due to a lack of competitors, they had eliminated the 150-pound weight division. If I still wanted to fight, I'd have to fight in the 170-pound division. For a moment, I considered asking for my fifty dollars back and getting started on the ten-hour drive home. Instead, I began pumping myself up. "So what if your opponent is a little bigger?" I said to myself. "If you get into trouble, just stick to what you know. You're one of the meanest wrestlers around, and if worst comes to worst, you can just hold him down until the end of the fight. You know you can do that, right? You know you can hold him down."

It was still several hours before the event got underway, but Lowell led me to the locker room to get changed. Every so often, I would sneak into the auditorium to watch the crowd coming in. In what seemed like no time at all, hundreds of seats were filled, and all eyes were focused on the elevated cage. That's when I began to get nervous. Never in my life had I competed before a crowd this large, and never had I put so much on the line. In wrestling, you win or lose by points. In mixed martial arts competition, you win or lose according to how much punishment and pain you can endure.

When the first fight of the night got started, I began warming up by grappling with Lowell. Slowly, I felt my confidence return. I was sure that what happened in all of my bouts would happen tonight: my wrestling skills would pull me through. Wrestlers did the best takedowns, the best sprawls, and they could outlast practitioners of any other discipline on the ground. No matter how skilled my opponents were on their feet, I would pull them down into my world.

Shortly before I was called on deck, Lowell pulled me aside for a little pep talk. "Now, I know what you're planning to do," he said, "and you can't do it. You have to forget your wrestling while you're out there. You have to forget everything you've ever done on the wrestling mats."

All at once, my tension returned, knotting the muscles in my neck. "What the hell are you talking about?" I demanded.

"Anyone can take his opponent down and pound on him," he answered. "John Perretti is in the broadcasters' booth—I just saw him. The only way you're going to make an impression on him is by fighting on your feet. You have to stand up and beat the crap out of your opponent with your hands. That's the only way you'll ever get to the UFC. You have to knock this guy out, you hear me! You have to knock him out!"

A few seconds later, someone was calling my name and telling me that it was my turn to fight. As much as

I hated Lowell for giving me that bit of news right before my match, I knew that he was right. And besides, I knew what my fists could do—I had unleashed them in bars all over Boise after I'd dropped out of school. I just wasn't sure what they could do in a UFC cage fight before an audience of thousands; and I hadn't stood up for a single one of my challenge matches. But if there was ever a time to throw some heavy leather, it was now.

As I made my way down a spectator-lined aisle of the auditorium on my way to the cage, I said to myself, "Unleash the devil inside of you. Make your opponent sorry for ever stepping into the cage with you. You better hurt him, because he's going to try to hurt you!"

Once the cage was locked, I found myself staring into the eyes of my first opponent, Curtis Hill. I couldn't hear the roar of the crowd. I couldn't hear Lowell coaching me from the corner. I was focused entirely on Hill, feeding off the energy that crackled in this calm before the storm.

The referee's hand slashed the air, and I moved forward until we were only a couple of feet apart. Then I let my left hand fly. It collided with Hill's cheek just below his right eye, my knuckles mashing through soft flesh until they struck bone. Even before I saw the pain twist his features into a terrible grimace, I knew that I'd hurt him. I'd had the same feeling while playing baseball as a child. When I cracked the ball just right, I didn't need to see it soaring over the outfield fence to know that I'd just batted a home run.

The impact of my fist made Hill stagger and fall. As I watched his body pitch forward, I was thinking, "Man, I just dropped him!" But when his body hit the canvas, I realized that the fight wasn't over. I could hear Lowell screaming at me from my corner, ordering me to finish what I'd started. So I leaped upon my downed foe and began tearing into his face with punches.

Curtis Hill was a worthy competitor, and he recovered quickly. While I was delivering countless hooks to his face, he summoned all of his strength and tried to shake me off. But I rode out his bucking and thrashing, continuing my assault. Growing desperate, he planted his hands on the canvas to get more leverage. That's when I dropped two knees to his jaw.

There was no doubt in my mind that I was ahead on the judges' cards. I knew that I could hold Hill down for the rest of the bout, nailing him with the occasional knee or elbow. Victory, however, wasn't my only goal. I had come to make an impression, and Lowell's words—"You have to knock this guy out, you hear me!"—echoed in my head. So I hopped back onto my feet, releasing Hill. He rose, I circled him for a few moments, and then bam!—I hit him again with a hard left, sending him onto his back once more. This time, I didn't even follow him down. My plan was to punish him from a standing position, and that's exactly what I did.

When I sent Curtis crashing to the canvas for the fourth time, his crew threw in the towel. In front of John Perretti and thousands of fans, I had won my first match of the night, and in a big way. As Lowell escorted me back to the locker room, I had a huge smile on my face. I couldn't believe I had defeated my opponent so easily, and what was even more incredible, I had defeated him with my fists. All I could do was stare at my hands and wonder how I could have neglected them for so long.

An hour later, as I fought David Harris in the finals, I got to see just what my fists were capable of. The crowd went wild as I beat Harris from one side of the cage to the other, hitting him with lefts, rights, knees, and elbows. Five minutes into the fight, I was thinking, "There's no way John Perretti isn't impressed." The problem was, I found myself thinking the same thing ten minutes into the fight, and then fifteen minutes into the fight. Soon, I was down to my last ounce of strength, and I started asking myself how this kid could still be standing. I hit him with everything I had, yet he refused to give up.

After dishing out punishment for twenty minutes, I abandoned my strategy of making an impression and went for the victory. When Harris threw a punch at my face, I ducked underneath him and took him down to the canvas. While both of us were struggling for position, he somehow got hold of my foot, but I wasn't the least bit worried because this allowed me to go for his neck. Unfortunately, I had no idea what a submissions expert could do to a foot.

While I was trying to wrap my arm around Harris's throat, a blinding pain shot from my toes all the way up to my thigh. Although I wasn't sure what was happening, I did know that something in my body was about to break. I was willing to push myself beyond my limits to earn the win, but I wasn't prepared to suffer a broken leg. Not knowing how to escape this predicament, I tapped my hand in submission.

A few moments later, after Harris's arm was raised above mine, I shook his hand and asked him what he had done. "Toe hold," he said with a smile. "I caught you in a toe hold."

Back in the locker room, I changed and packed my things as fast as I could. I didn't want to admit to anyone that I'd tapped out because of a toe hold. I wanted to get far away from the scene of my humiliating loss. But before I could slip out the back door unnoticed, John Perretti caught up with me and asked if we could talk.

"That was absolutely amazing," he said to me.

I looked at him in confusion and said, "Which bout are you talking about?"

"Both of them."

"But I lost . . ."

"Yeah, but you also showed some tremendous skill. I'm thinking about starting a new bantamweight division in the UFC, and I think you've got the talent to compete in it. But first you have to learn how to finish off your opponent once you've got him hurt. You've got heart and strength, but until you learn some finishing moves, you won't be UFC material. Why don't you go home and work on it, then come back at the next event? If I see that you've got the right stuff, then I'll see what I can do."

As Perretti wandered off to talk with some of the other fighters, I sat there speechless. Suddenly it all seemed worthwhile: the cuts, the bruises, the endless hours of training. As far as I was concerned, Perretti's words were as good as an invitation to compete in the UFC, because nothing was going to stand in my way. I would improve and learn some devastating finishing moves. I already felt sorry for the next son of a bitch to step into the cage with me.

When I got home, I immediately started working on my fighting skills. Because my schedule made it impossible for me to train at Lowell's gym, I rented a stack of UFC videos and began breaking down the moves of my idols. Once again, my teammates let me use their bodies for practice, and every day I found myself sleeker on the ground. It wasn't long before I could capture an opponent in any number of submissions, and if he somehow powered out of one, I would simply drop into the next.

By the time I got to the second Bas Rutten Invitational, I felt confident about my finishing moves, and I fought like the devil. I submitted my first opponent with a choke, and then I scored a one-punch KO in the finals, shattering my opponent's cheek and the fragile bones in my left hand. The prize money wouldn't even cover the hospital bill, but I didn't care.

Shortly after the event, Perretti told me that he was going to add me to the card of UFC XXII, to be

held on September 24, 1999, in Lake Charles, Louisiana. I would be competing in the first-ever bantamweight bout, and my opponent would be world-class
kick boxer and mixed martial artist Alfonso Alcarez.

14

UFC

Before I take you to the Ultimate Fighting Championships for the biggest fight of my life, let me take a step back in history and describe how the UFC—the extravaganza that forever changed the world's view of the martial arts—came to be.

It all started with one man's dream. Growing up in Brazil, Rorion Gracie had watched his father, Helio, dominate countless no-holds-barred challenge matches. With a unique brand of jiu-jitsu that focused on ground fighting and submission holds, Helio defeated boxing, karate, and kung fu practitioners, making the name of Gracie famous throughout Brazil. Although Helio's career as a fighter ended in 1957, Rorion had no intention of letting the family name fade into obscurity. In 1978, he moved to the United States to introduce the art of Gracie jiu-jitsu to the wider world.

But Rorion did not realize his vision of a jiu-jitsu martial arts empire right away. Americans had no idea what Brazilian jiu-jitsu was. They'd never heard of such powerful techniques as arm bars and ankle locks.

They didn't understand that a fighter lying on his back could actually be in an advantageous position. Shortly after Rorion arrived in the Land of Opportunity, he discovered that no one was interested in seeing him prove that his family's system of jiu-jitsu was the most effective fighting style around. Swayed by the romantic mysticism of movies like Bruce Lee's *Enter the Dragon*, Americans wanted to learn how to perform flashy kicks and open-hand strikes.

Frustrated but not defeated, Rorion spent the next ten years teaching his family art out of his Hermosa Beach, California, garage to anyone who was interested. When a new student showed up to take a class, he'd invite him into the house and show him tapes of Gracie family members fighting in matches back home in Brazil. Rorion had fifteen such tapes, and each time he showed them he had to explain the action. One day, he decided to simplify the process by joining the fight tapes together and overlaying a narrative. Rorion marketed the tape, entitled *Gracies in Action*, advertising it in martial arts magazines. Slowly, word of Gracie jiu-jitsu began to spread through the fight world.

But Rorion wanted to capture the attention of the general public as well. In order to do this, he invited three of his brothers—Rickson, Royce, and Royler—to America in 1989 to help him open a school in Torrance, California. The school, called the Gracie Academy, did raise the profile of Gracie jiu-jitsu, but Rorion didn't stop there. He was convinced that people all over the United States would be interested in learning his art, so he put together a series of instructional videotapes. To sell the tapes, he employed one of his students, Art Davie.

In 1992, having just quit his job at an advertising agency, Art Davie was looking for a new project. Intrigued by the Gracie family's skill, he signed up for classes at the academy. When Rorion asked him to market the instructional videos and *Gracies in Action*, he was happy to do it. He sold them via direct mail, and they were a tremendous hit. Inspired by this success, Davie started dreaming up a Gracie jiu-jitsu media extravaganza. He wanted to create a show that captured the reality-based essence of the Gracie challenge by pitting practitioners of different martial arts disciplines against one another in a no-rules environment.

Rorion knew that his family members would prevail in such an event because they had been doing so for almost a century in Brazil. It was the perfect way to prove the effectiveness of his art, so he immediately began searching for a way to bring the event to life. Working with Davie, he wrote a detailed proposal and began pitching the idea to the established pay-per-view companies, but it didn't get a positive response. Finally, the proposal fell into the hands of someone at Semaphore Entertainment Group who had enough insight to see its potential. Within a few months, the first Ultimate Fighting Championships event was on the drawing board.

Neither Rorion Gracie nor Art Davie had any idea how popular the event was going to be. Because they didn't even know whether the event would draw an audience, they marketed the UFC as a bloody spectacle in order to generate some media hype. They boasted that there were no rules, and that victory could come in the form of knockout, submission, or even death.

When the first UFC was broadcast to homes around the world, on December 11, 1993, no one knew what to expect. But over the next hour and a half, thousands of martial arts fans watched Royce Gracie, Rorion's chosen family representative, take his opponents to the canvas and wrap himself around them like a snake. Without throwing a single worthy punch, he defeated expert strikers and shattered the mysticism that surrounded the Eastern fighting styles.

Traditional martial artists offered a thousand explanations for why Royce had won the competition. But then Royce went ahead and mowed down all of his opponents during the second Ultimate Fighting Championships, held on November 3, 1994, and any doubts about Gracie jiu-jitsu still lingering in the fight world were swept away. Soon, the Gracie Academy was inundated with students. Rorion busily sold T-shirts, videotapes, and Gracie paraphernalia, turning the family art into a multimillion-dollar business. The Gracie family became world-renowned. Rorion had finally realized his dream.

Determined to maintain the momentum, Rorion held one event after another. The UFC became the fastest-growing pay-per-view event of all time, and enthusiasts everywhere were scrambling to learn Gracie jiu-jitsu. Submissions schools popped up all over the United States, and practitioners began blending their striking with grappling, giving birth to a hybrid fighting style and the sport of mixed martial arts.

Despite its popularity, the UFC did have its share of critics. The most powerful of these critics was Republican senator John McCain, who just so happened to be married to the heiress of Budweiser, boxing's biggest sponsor. Those involved in the sport of boxing had grown increasingly worried that this new form of combative entertainment would erode their own fan base, so they deployed an influential politician to help defuse the threat.

On December 6, 1995, McCain appeared on *Larry King Live* to express his distaste for mixed martial arts competition. He even went so far as to say that it "appeals to the lowest common denominator in our society"; then he announced that he was going to do whatever it took to get those vile UFC broadcasts off the air. He actually accomplished this goal by convincing the cable giants to drop their coverage of reality-fighting events. UFC XII, held on July 12, 1996, was the last UFC event to be seen by the mainstream viewing public. Although diehard fans could still watch their favorite warriors duke it out on video, the money behind the sport was gone, and even the best fighters in the business found themselves laying it on the line for next to nothing.

While some UFC fighters went on to compete in the rings of Japan, and still others crossed over into the lucrative field of professional wrestling, many chose to stick it out and perfect their skills in the hope that one day their sport would regain the spotlight. But as time passed, the future looked bleaker and bleaker.

By the time UFC XXII rolled around—the event at which I was slated to make my first Octagon appearance—my chances of making a living as a reality fighter were slim. In order to compete at that level, I'd have to drop all of my other pursuits and devote myself totally to the sport. The risk level was high. I needed money to eat, pay the rent, and finish school, and if I gambled on winning and then lost, I'd be in serious trouble. I could easily imagine myself back in Seattle living in another ghetto apartment. But if I put mixed martial arts competition on the back burner and just trained whenever I had the chance, then I'd likely blow my only shot at becoming a mixed martial arts champion.

In the end, risk or no risk, I decided that I couldn't pass up this opportunity. I longed to be a champion.

15

Debut

A few weeks after the Bas Rutten Invitational, I sat on the couch in my Boise apartment and thought about the monumental opportunity that stood before me: in less than a month, I was scheduled to compete in the UFC—the most famous mixed martial arts competition in the world.

The problem was, grappling with my fellow wrestlers and driving up to train with Lowell once every two weeks wasn't enough to prepare me to meet the challenge I faced. Every other athlete competing in the UFC had spent thousands of hours in the gym learning countless ways to submit their opponents. They were experts at punching, kicking, and grappling. They had honed their skills in numerous smaller competitions and proven their abilities as universal fighters. By the time they entered the Octagon, they had transformed themselves into members of the world's fighting elite. They were ready to compete in the most realistic hand-to-hand competition on the planet.

I didn't want to make a fool of myself by showing up unprepared and falling victim to something as ridiculous as a toe hold. I didn't want to get my face kicked in on pay-per-view either. It was clear to me that to get the training I needed I'd have to leave Boise. Before I could show the world the real Jens Pulver, I had to train with people who were better than me, people who could show me whether I had what it took to overcome adversity and rise to any occasion.

So I picked up the phone and called Bob Shamrock, founder of the world-renowned Lion's Den training facility. Bob was the father of Ken and Frank Shamrock, two fighters who had dominated the Octagon since the UFC's inception. Together, the brothers had fought all over the world—Japan, Brazil, Europe, the United States—and destroyed opponents from practically every martial arts discipline. During every event, Bob had been on the sidelines to coach his boys through. I figured that if Bob would allow me onto his newly formed team, Shamrock 2000, and share with me the expertise he had developed through his years in the fight game, then I'd have it made.

"Who will you be fighting?" Bob asked after I'd introduced myself and explained my situation.

"Alfonso Alcarez."

"The kick boxer?"

"Yeah, I think so."

"The guy's a strong striker, so you're going to have your work cut out for you. I can get some tapes of his fights for us to study, but until then you'll need to do cardio, weight lifting, and practice your submissions."

"I have a strong wrestling background," I told him, "but I need to learn more submissions."

"Nothing to worry about. I've got the perfect guy for you. His name is Valerie Ignatov—as a matter of fact, he'll be fighting in the same UFC as you. He's a Bulgarian sambo champion, and a Russian sambo champion, and he's currently rated number two in the world. He can teach you a hundred different leg locks and submissions. Now, I don't want to blow smoke up your ass. If you want to get asked back to the UFC, you're going to have to win, and the only way you can do that is by training your ass off."

As I listened to Bob Shamrock talk, I felt emotions well up inside of me. Here, at last, was the man I had been looking for, the man who could tell me how things were. Right off the bat, I knew that he was my next Russ Hayden or Dan Staab. When Bob finished his pep talk, he told me that if I still thought Shamrock 2000 could help me, then he would fly me out to his place in Lodi, California, whenever I was ready.

I packed my bags that evening, but when I lay down to get a good night's rest, a million thoughts started racing through my head. I thought of Kelly, of fishing in the river, of all the friends who continued to support me. I also thought about Lowell. I had called him right after I'd spoken to Bob. Now I replayed the conversation we'd had over and over in my mind. Lowell had called me a traitor because I was leaving his team now that things were good for me. I knew that I owed him—and the members of the Boise State wrestling team—a lot, but I also knew that my decision to join the Shamrock team was the right one. And any second thoughts I might have had were swept aside when I imagined myself doing battle in the Octagon, an octagonal ring surrounded by a six-foot chain-link fence, under a blaze of red and blue lights. This was the opportunity of a lifetime, and I had to do whatever it took to turn it into a triumph. I wasn't abandoning the people who'd helped me, because they would always hold a place in my heart. They fueled my warrior spirit, they sustained me as I moved slowly towards my dream.

Bob, an energetic man with gray hair and a huge grin, picked me up at the airport in Sacramento and drove me to Lodi, an agricultural community in California's central valley. The sprawling suburb looked too tame to have produced a number of the world's most accomplished athletes, but here Bob Shamrock had trained some of the best reality fighters in the business. Out of Lodi had come Jerry Bohlander, Pete Williams, and Mikey Burnett, to name just a few.

After taking me on a brief tour of Lodi's wine country, Bob brought me to Animal House Gym, the official training facility of Shamrock 2000. There, behind a pile of ancient weight-lifting equipment, was a ring, a mat, and several heavy bags. Although it wasn't what I'd expected—I had envisioned an expanse of cages and rows of strange strength-building devices straight out of a Rocky movie—I found myself smiling from ear to ear. It was an honor just to be in the gym where some of the world's top warriors had developed their skills.

For the next two weeks, I trained from sunup to sundown. I grappled with Valerie Ignatov as well as with Steve Heath, a ruthless brawler who had dominated the International Fighting Championships. I sparred with Cal Worsham, a UFC veteran who had defeated Zane Frazier and gone to war against the infamous Tank Abbott. I worked on submissions with old Lion's Den fighter Jason Pietz and muay Thai fighter Erich Krauss, a kick boxer who'd fought in the rings of Bangkok. Shamrock's outfit boasted a stellar cast, and as I pushed my body to the limit, my confidence slowly increased.

The week before I was to fly to Louisiana for my UFC debut, I felt more than prepared. I could grapple for thirty minutes straight without getting winded. I could punch as hard as a fighter twice my size. And, most importantly, I could count on having Bob Shamrock at my side to coach me through the biggest night of my life.

As my moment approached, I wasn't nervous. I didn't get nervous until I stood in the back of Lake Charles Civic Auditorium looking down at the famous, brilliantly lit Octagon. The alcohol-laced body heat of twelve thousand fight fans hit me in the face like the back of a hand. The Octagon looked far more menacing than it did on television. Even from where I stood, high above the fighting pit, I could see rust-colored stains on the canvas where warriors had fallen in painful defeat. And, as if that wasn't nerve-racking enough, positioned around the perimeter of the Octagon were a dozen television cameras training their dark, mechanical eyes on the site of the action. They reminded me of the millions of people watching at home, waiting for me to fail. Bob was telling me to relax and breathe, but my heart was pounding faster and faster. Whatever happened in the next half hour, I knew that I'd never be the same again.

The UFC's theme song echoed through the auditorium, and I began my descent. I kept my eyes pinned to the ground as spectators reached over the guardrail to pat me on the back. I didn't look up until I was locked inside the Octagon, and then I found myself staring into the face of Alfonso Alcarez.

He was a five-foot-seven mountain of muscle with a barrel chest and legs as thick as tree trunks. I immediately began searching for his weak point, the place where I could strike him over and over until he was wheezing with pain, but before I could find it, I heard the words I'd heard a hundred times before on television: "Let's get it on!"

Without thinking it through, I did what I did best. I shot in and took my opponent to the mat. My body scrambling on top of his, I could feel his strength and the memory came to me of my back-and-forth battle with Lenox Morris in high school. In order to beat Alcarez, I would have to use my head instead of my physical power. I had to outmaneuver him, outposition him, and when I had him where I wanted him, I had to unload my strikes.

Before I could get into an advantageous position, however, Alcarez managed to turn over and get on all fours. Knowing he was dangerous on his feet, I kept him down with the weight of my body while unleashing a series of knees to his face. They weren't knockout shots, but they were enough to make him uncomfortable. Just as he was starting to cover up, I wrapped my arm around his neck and went for a guillotine choke—one of the many finishing moves I had perfected during my stint in California.

It was then that I truly felt the strength Alcarez possessed. He powered out of my hold with ease and lumbered to his feet. Before he could find his balance, however, I fired on him with uppercuts and jabs. Landing those blows, I felt much the way I had when I struck Curtis Hill at the first Bas Rutten Invitational. With each fist that crashed into Alcarez's face, I saw that baseball soaring higher over the outfield.

So I just kept banging on him with everything I had, thinking that at any minute he would drop. But UFC competitors like Alcarez had weathered worse storms than this. Despite the punishment I was dishing out, Bob knew that my opponent could come back in a sudden flurry. "Tie up!" he shouted. "Tie up with him!"

I wasn't about to disregard the advice of the man who, on many occasions, had coached Ken Shamrock to victory in this very Octagon, so I cupped my hands around Alcarez's face and delivered knee after crushing knee to his midsection. One knee contacted his sternum, the air rushed out of his lungs, and he buckled. This filled me with confidence, and without hesitation I continued the assault, only this time the knees I threw were landing to his face. By the time the first round was over, Alcarez was little more than my punching bag.

When I staggered back to my corner, exhausted from throwing all that leather, Bob told me to stay calm and not burn myself out. I listened to his words, but one idea flashed like a neon sign in my mind: I had to knock Alcarez out. I wanted this win to be decisive. When I stepped out of the cage, I didn't want anyone to have lingering doubts about who had won.

Alcarez, however, had different plans. Although his face had been punched and kneed and his lungs felt like they were going to collapse, his determination to win was as strong as it was when the fight began. At the opening of the second round, he came at me like a train, catching me off guard. Before I had time to retaliate or defend, he delivered several uppercuts to my jaw.

The shots pissed me off more than anything, and I plowed him forward and trapped him against the fence. Again I began chopping away at him with my knees, only now he was fighting back, hooking to my body and head. At one point, he managed to pick me up and toss me over his back, but by that time I realized there wasn't anything he could do to hurt me.

With only minutes left in the bout, both of us went wild. I continued slamming knees into his chest, and he continued throwing hooks to my head. At one point, we tore into each other for a solid minute, then Alcarez ducked low and snatched my legs, pulling me onto my back. This appeared to be a disadvantageous position for me, but I continued my assault, jabbing up at him, past his swinging fists, until the buzzer sounded.

Returning to my corner, I was greeted not only by Bob, but also by John Perretti. "That was an incredible fight!" Perretti shouted. "Man, what an incredible fight!" I thanked him, then I turned to Bob and whispered, "Did I win?" He looked at me and smiled. "You won without a doubt."

I was still breathing heavily when the referee pulled me over to the middle of the Octagon. Bob's confidence meant the world to me, but I could only hope that the judges felt the way he did. What happened in the next few moments would determine the next ten years of my life. I knew I'd given the crowd a good show, but there were hundreds of worthy fighters trying to get into the UFC, and if I lost this bout it might be years before they would allow me back into the event. If I won, however, I would have the chance to make a career of fighting.

The fans fell silent as the announcer prepared to read the judges' decision. My chest was still heaving. I could hear my heart pounding in my ears. Out of the corner of my eye, I could see Alcarez. I wanted to pat him on the back. We had gone to war against each other, but now that all the punches had been thrown, we could be friends. He was as tough as they come, and he'd handled everything I could muster.

A moment later, cameras flashing around me, I felt my hand rise into the air. Then tears were streaming down my cheeks. It was the greatest victory I had ever known.

But before I even had a chance to celebrate with Bob and my Shamrock 2000 teammates, my triumph was snatched away from me. Although my win had been announced to the thousands in attendance, half an hour after the fight, UFC officials came to the locker room to notify Bob that the judgment had been changed. They had declared the match a draw.

Fuming, Bob went to argue it out with John Perretti, but Perretti was just as appalled. Apparently, the event's promoters thought that the fight had gone so well that they should schedule a rematch. And they figured the best way to publicize that rematch would be to promote it as a grudge match.

In the days that followed, having my win pulled wasn't the only blow I suffered. As I have already mentioned, the cable ban was taking its toll on UFC promoters, and that trickled down to the various teams, including Shamrock 2000. Fighters' purses were dwindling with each event, and Shamrock 2000 wasn't earning enough money to stay afloat. Shortly after I returned home, Bob called to tell me that the team was disbanding. Although it hurt him to let me and the rest of his fighters go, he could do nothing about it.

I was now in a bind. With my next UFC appearance just around the corner, I had to go searching for a
new place to train, a place where I could get the help I
needed to maintain the skills I'd acquired and improve
on them as well. But Bob Shamrock came through for
me—he wasn't about to leave me high and dry. He did
me the huge favor of telling me about Pat Miletich
and Monte Cox.

16

Road of Champions

A decade before me, in Iowa, Pat Miletich had become involved in the sport of mixed martial arts. Like me, he'd started out as a wrestler. When his wrestling career came to an end after college, he discovered that he still thirsted for competition, so he decided to learn how to fight. He started off with kick boxing, and his record grew to an amazing twelve and zero.

But upon seeing Royce Gracie dominate the UFC with his jiu-jitsu skills, Miletich realized that his own fighting system was far from complete, and he began to learn submissions. Just as he was fine-tuning a system of fighting that meshed his striking with his grappling abilities, a friend named Tom Letulli asked him to compete in a mixed martial arts competition he was putting on in Chicago called Battle of the Masters. Although it was an eight-man elimination tournament, Miletich felt confident that he could win.

Hoping to get some press for both the sport and his own career, Miletich contacted Monte Cox, a reporter for his local newspaper, the *Quad City Times* of Davenport, Iowa. Although Cox had been an ama-teur boxer himself and had even promoted boxing matches for networks such as ESPN and USA, he knew absolutely nothing about mixed martial arts and cage fighting. Miletich filled him in on Battle of the Mas-ters, but Cox insisted on seeing for himself what the sport was all about before he wrote an article on it.

After visiting Miletich at his gym and seeing first-hand that mixed martial arts combatants were far from the barbarians Senator John McCain was making them out to be, Cox was intrigued and decided to witness Miletich in action at the Battle of the Masters. Miletich ran through the competition, easily defeating opponents fifty pounds heavier than he was. Cox was hooked. A short while later, he started hosting his own mixed martial arts show, which he dubbed the Quad City Ultimate.

The first such show was held on January 20, 1996, in Davenport's Mark of the Quad Cities, a ten-thousand-seat venue. It was a tremendous success, and, before eight thousand spectators, Iowa's very own Pat Miletich won both of his bouts.

The success of this first endeavor made Cox eager to mount more such events. Despite the fact that he entered the scene right when political pressures were making a mess of it, Cox went on to stage almost 140 mixed martial arts competitions over a five-year period—the most popular of these was the Extreme Challenge. While many fighters and promoters were dropping out of the sport because of the cable ban,

Cox and Miletich thrived. They became leaders in training, promotion, and management. As far as they were concerned, the hard years were behind them and the future was bright.

Needless to say, once I learned about Cox's and Miletich's histories in the sport of mixed martial arts, I was very impressed. They knew the game like no one else did, and they had created dozens of champions. Miletich could offer me the training that I needed at his Miletich Fighting Systems facility; and Cox could ensure that promoters never robbed me of my prize money or reversed the judges' decisions on me. If I could get such an experienced pair to take me on, then nothing could stop me from realizing my dream.

So, after I learned that Shamrock 2000 was disbanding, I got on the horn and called Monte Cox. I told him what I needed, and before our conversation ended he invited me to come out to Iowa and see what I thought.

"I don't need to see it," I told him. "If you'll have me, then that's where I want to be."

I began packing my things, as excited as I'd ever been. It wasn't until three days later, when I was standing at the Boise train station with my two duffel bags, that I began to have second thoughts. Once again, I was leaving Boise not knowing when I'd be able to return. While I was building a fighting career in Iowa, things would be changing in my adopted hometown. The people I loved would move ahead with their lives, and I wouldn't be a part of it. Boise would slowly fade in my memory; I'd recall it only when I was feeling blue. I hated the thought, yet a hunger inside me made me grit my teeth and board that eastbound train.

For two days I traveled, watching the American landscape flow by. The seats next to me were vacant, so I spent the time in silence. I experienced the same emotions I'd felt when I traveled to Boise for the first time, and I remembered how my gut had twisted in excitement at the thought of becoming an all-American wrestler and a national champion. I was young then. I had wasted that opportunity, but now another stood in front of me. Most people don't get a first chance to realize their dreams, let alone a second one or a third one. I considered myself to be the luckiest son of a bitch alive, and I vowed to do things right this time. The UFC's 150-pound weight division was wide open, and I planned to make a huge impact there—a gigantic statement. I was going to carve my name into history.

When the train finally came screeching into the Davenport station, I felt like I had landed in a foreign territory. Flat, lonely agricultural land spread out forever in all directions, and the sky was an overcast gray. I immediately longed for Idaho. But before I became overwhelmed by it all, I reminded myself that I'd come here for a reason, grabbed a taxi, and headed for the gym where I would soon be spending my every waking minute.

Pat Miletich didn't have a labyrinth of high-tech equipment; neither did he own the building that housed his training facility. He taught his young scrappers the art of reality fighting in a disused racquetball court in a local gym. Worn-out wrestling mats covered the floor and walls, and a single punching bag hung in a corner. That was pretty much it. But as I stood looking down on a practice though the spectator's window, what I saw practically took my breath away. The court was brimming with fighters, some of whom I had been watching for years on television.

In one corner, Jeremy Horn was working on his stand-up, going toe to toe with a guy twice his size. On the mats, Matt Hughes, future UFC champion of the world, was throwing someone around like a rag doll, perfecting the slam that would soon drive fight fans into a frenzy. And watching over them all, correcting their form and making suggestions, was Pat Miletich, the current UFC welterweight champion who'd defended his title against the world's best for the previous four years.

A moment later, Miletich spotted me and motioned for me to come down to the practice. Ten minutes after that, I was on the mats, grappling with one submissions expert after another. Most of my opponents were bigger than I was, but they still came at me with everything they had. I got caught in headlocks and front chokes, and every two minutes I found myself pounding my hand in submission. By the time that practice was over, I was angry and humiliated. I wanted to get back on the train and head home to Boise. But I couldn't deny that this was exactly what I'd come to Iowa for. I knew that I needed to get beat down, stepped on, and humiliated in order to learn. And if I was ever going to become the best 150-pound fighter in the world, then I had to learn. Experience had taught me that only by losing every day at practice could I win in the ring.

So, on a daily basis, I suffered the sting of defeat. To make matters worse, my living situation was also an exercise in humility. I'd arrived in Iowa with less than a hundred dollars, so renting my own apartment was an impossibility. Monte Cox let me stay at his house, and although I had a blast living under the same roof as my manager, it wasn't my own place. I was scraping by on next to nothing, living off the generosity of my team.

I refused to let all of this get me down. Instead, I turned it into fuel for the fire. I told myself that I'd have to earn everything that I wanted, and in a way it was a romantic notion. Starting with nothing, I'd rebuild my life from the ground up. Although my teammates, coach, and manager were lending me a hand, I still had to make it on my own. I was constructing my future, one day at a time.

Those first few months, I practically lived in the gym. After the afternoon practice, when all the other fighters were at home in their apartments, I bedded down in a corner of the gym, resting my body so I could come back strong for the evening session. And when training was over for the day, I didn't go out and socialize. I didn't do anything but eat, sleep, and breathe fighting.

My teammates began to think I was nuts for pushing myself so hard. But no matter how tired or lazy they were feeling, I tore into them at practice and demanded that they do the same in return. After a few months of this, they began calling me "Little Evil." Although most of the time my new nickname cropped up in sentences like, "Man, you're a little evil bastard," I took it as a compliment. It reminded me that for once I wasn't wasting a golden opportunity.

Each day, I became more of an asset to the team. I pushed other fighters to their limits to prepare them for their upcoming bouts. I learned new submissions and how to escape from them. I turned my body into a machine and waited for my chance to shine.

Although Iowa became my ultimate workshop, I still didn't consider it home. In the mornings, I'd watch fly-fishing competitions on television to keep up with the techniques. I talked constantly about the mountains, the rivers, and all the friends I'd left behind in Idaho. I longed to realize my dream so I could return home. As the months passed, my memories of Idaho didn't fade as I'd expected they would—they grew stronger.

By the end of my first year in Davenport, a lot had happened to me. For UFC XXIV, held on March 10, 2000, I returned to the Octagon to put my new skills to the test against Dave Velasquez, who was a member of Frank Shamrock's newly formed team. Despite Velasquez's experience, I wasn't intimidated. I beat him in every possible way for two minutes and forty-one seconds, then the referee put an end to the abuse. Riding on the momentum, I went to UFC XXVI, held on June 9, 2000, and earned a judges' decision after dominating my opponent, Joao Roque.

Although my Octagon victories brought me all the glory and honor I thought they would, the thing that had the biggest impact in my life that year was not related to fighting. After focusing all my attention on training for eight months straight, I started allowing myself a little leisure time. Every once in a while I'd go out for an evening, and one night I met a girl named Gina. We dated for several weeks, and then she took me home to meet her family. Her parents were farmers, and their lives revolved around planting and harvesting crops. They were good people with good hearts, and I guess that's why I was so deeply affected when Gina introduced me to her cousin Dusty and told me that he'd been stricken with cancer and didn't have long to live.

Dusty was only seventeen years old. He dreamed of farming like the rest of his family, but he was never going to get that chance. The fact that he would be robbed of his life before he ever got to live it pissed me off at first, but then it sent me into a depression. How could the world work like that? How could I be allowed one chance after another to achieve my goals while Dusty never got a single opportunity? What made me so special? I had walked a hard road, but it was nothing like the one Dusty was walking in the last months of his life. When I was a child, I often woke up wondering if today would be my last day on earth, but I'd always had a ray of hope. Dusty didn't have any hope. The cancer was eating away at him from the inside, and nothing could postpone his death.

I thought a lot about mortality in those few months that I spent hanging out with Gina and Dusty. I reflected on how lucky I was to be able to compete and experience glory, and I decided that I wanted Dusty to experience it through me. When I got the news that I would be fighting John Lewis, my toughest opponent to date, in UFC XXVIII, I resolved to dedicate the fight to Dusty. I wanted to give him hope, if only for a fleeting moment. It was important to me that all those people watching on pay-per-view hear Dusty's name. Before he went away, I wanted to give him one victory, no matter how insignificant it was.

I stepped into the Octagon on fight night sensing that this match was the most important one I'd ever fought. Dusty was watching at home, and I had to put everything I had into it right from the start. I'd give him something to think about as he lay in bed—something to dream about.

When Lewis came at me jabbing in the opening seconds of the bout, I moved forward, slipped his punches, and threw a huge left hook to his chin. I hit him harder than I had ever hit anyone. He fell to the canvas and didn't get up. The fight was over in thirty-five seconds.

I ran from one side of the cage to the other, looking for a camera to send my words back to Iowa. Finding one, I shouted, "This one is for you, Dusty!"

A few months later, I went to Gina's parents' house for Thanksgiving, and after dinner we played a tape of the fight. These were people who rarely displayed their emotions, but when the fight was over they cried and told me how grateful they were. I told them that I was the grateful one—I was grateful to Dusty. He had changed my life in the short time I'd known him. Because of him, I'd taken time out from my relentless quest and learned the important lesson that it's the small things in life that matter most.

Although my relationship with Gina didn't work out, Dusty remained in my thoughts. After my fight with John Lewis, people wanted to know more about Dusty—who he was and where he was from. I was scheduled to fight Caol Uno for the bantamweight title belt at UFC XXX, and on that occasion I planned to tell the world just how much Dusty meant to me. I assumed Dusty himself would be watching at home.

Things didn't turn out that way, however. Only four days before the match, Dusty passed away. I tried to put it out of my mind for the duration of the fight, but everything came crashing down the moment I set foot in the Octagon. Announcer Bruce Beck, unaware that his voice was being broadcast throughout the arena, began telling the pay-per-view audience about Dusty. He said, "Let me tell you something about Jens Pulver. He dedicated his last victory inside the Octagon to young Dusty, and Dusty carried that tape around for a long time. Dusty was a seventeen year old who was terminally ill with cancer, and he died last Thursday. Young Jens Pulver told me before the fight yesterday . . . he told me that God decided that he would rather have Dusty in the ring with me tonight than watching on TV. Go get 'em, Jens."

Hearing Dusty's name over the loudspeakers brought tears to my eyes. I couldn't control them, so I turned my back to the cameras and wiped my eyes. To some, those tears may have seemed a sign of weakness, but for me they were a sign of strength. I truly meant what I had said to Bruce Beck. Standing in the Octagon, living the moment that I had been anticipating for so long, I knew that Dusty was by my side. We were going to win the belt together.

I fought better than I'd ever fought before. Uno had defeated the world's top competitors, and he had come prepared for all-out war. He took me down to the canvas, searching for one submission after another. At one point, he even got my back and wrapped his arm around my throat in an attempt to choke me out. But no matter what he did, I didn't let him intimidate me, because I had someone with me, giving me strength. I dealt with everything Uno could dish out, and then I retaliated with my thunderous left hand. By the beginning of the fourth round, Uno had absorbed so much punishment that he began falling to the canvas with the hope of coaxing me down there with him. I refused to join him. Announcer Jeff Blatnick was right on the money when he said, "Pulver seems to be asserting his will in the standing position."

The last round came to a close, and those powerful emotions hit me once again. When a camera swung around to my face, I said, "I'm glad you were in there with me, buddy. I talked to you the whole time." It was the truth—Dusty had carried me through that twenty-five-minute war. When the judges' decision came back and the title belt was strapped around my waist, I felt utterly fulfilled. I had given up my life in Boise to go to Davenport, where I'd endured loneliness and some nasty weather. I had gambled everything, and I'd come out on top. From that moment forward, I would always be a champion. I had attained the highest level in the sport, and no one could ever take that away from me—and Dusty.

After becoming an official champion of the UFC, the only thing I had left to do was defend my title. Matt Hughes once told me that you're not a real champion until you do that, and after much consideration I agreed with him. Anyone can win the belt on a given day, but keeping it is an entirely different matter. Once you're under the gun—once everyone wants what you have—the going gets tough. That's when you have to step up and prove that you deserved the belt. So, after beating Caol Uno, my next goal became to show everyone that my win was no fluke.

I had no idea how difficult that would be.

17

A Threat on the Horizon

While I was growing up, my father told me a thousand times that I was destined to fail. The idea was ingrained in me. I was worthless and weak, he insisted, and if I dared to disagree, he'd prove his point by laying into me with his fists. I was taught to hate myself, to hate the person I was bound to become. For years, I believed my father's every word, but then I discovered wrestling, and everything changed. By the time I graduated from high school, I was dead set on proving my father wrong by achieving greatness.

I suffered my share of defeats, but over the years I also racked up numerous victories. I had won state and national wrestling titles. I had built a group of friends, I'd had productive relationships, and I'd held a steady job. Although I considered all of these accomplishments noteworthy, nothing compared with the euphoria of becoming a world champion. The moment I was awarded the Ultimate Fighting Championships lightweight title belt, I finally overturned my father's negative prediction. I was Little Evil, and the fear of failure had been washed from every recess of my mind.

But that all changed on November 2, 2001.

Thanks to all the loyal fans and Zuffa Sports Entertainment, the UFC had reentered the spotlight. Zuffa had bought the enterprise, and they pumped millions into advertising. They also managed to get the Nevada State Athletic Commission to sanction their events and get the major cable companies to lift their ban. UFC XXXIV, held at the MGM Grand Hotel and Casino in Las Vegas, was the second show back on pay-per-view. Along with improving production values, the new management had also arranged for some new commentators—at every show, one of the fighters would sit in the broadcast booth and give a blow-by-blow account of the action occurring in the Octagon.

Plenty of fighters were willing to serve as commentator—some more articulate than others. But they asked me, which was a great honor, because UFC XXXIV was one of the biggest shows to date. I agreed, of course. Arriving at the MGM Grand, I was ready to tell it as I saw it. While Josh Barnett tackled Bobby Hoffman and Matt Lindland exchanged blows with Phil Baroni, I interjected my two cents' worth.

Despite my enthusiasm, I was a bit preoccupied during the preliminary fights. Caol Uno was scheduled to fight B. J. Penn in the third bout of the night, and the winner would get a shot at my title belt in the next event. This was my chance to study them both and learn just who and what I was up against.

I wasn't concerned about Uno. Although the twenty-five-minute back-and-forth battle we'd waged in UFC XXX had been the toughest of my life, I knew that if we faced off again, my victory would be a lot swifter. After years of grappling with the same series of wrestlers in countless competitions, I had learned that once I'd defeated a guy, he was doomed. It had happened with Lenox Morris. He chewed through me twice in a row, but then I beat him, and he no longer stood a chance.

It was B. J. Penn who occupied my thoughts. Although he didn't look like a threat, his record was intimidating. In 1999, he'd gone to Brazil and become the first foreigner to win the jiu-jitsu world championships. He had a vast arsenal of submissions, and after getting defeated by a toe hold in the Bas Rutten Invitational, I knew just how dangerous a submissions expert could be.

Despite Penn's jiu-jitsu accomplishments, when he first applied to fight in the UFC, many critics—UFC matchmakers included—thought he'd get trucked over in a competition where striking was allowed. Still, the UFC agreed to give him a chance, and in UFC XXXI he proved just how well-rounded he was. His opponent was Joey Gilbert, my old college roommate. Penn took Gilbert to the canvas, mounted his back, and unleashed a series of devastating hooks to the head that forced the referee to call a halt to the fight. With this impressive debut under his belt, Penn reentered the Octagon in UFC XXXII and knocked Din Thomas out cold with a single knee to the jaw. Penn was quoted as saying, "Although I'm always looking for a submission, I simply like to hit people." He'd been fighting in the streets all of his life.

However, the tricks he'd learned in back-alley scraps wouldn't help him much against a world-class veteran like Caol Uno. Regardless of all the B. J. Penn hype, I was certain Uno would be victorious. He had fought some of the toughest warriors on the planet, myself included, and I'd never seen him get knocked out. He was quick and strong, and he could escape from almost any submission.

Sitting ringside in the broadcasters' booth, I eagerly awaited the Penn-Uno bout, and when the two light-weights finally entered the Octagon I stared at them, trying to read their expressions. As the referee reiterated the rules, I was more certain than ever that Uno would be the one I'd have to face at the next UFC. He was calm and collected; Penn pranced back and forth, working himself up. From my years of experience I knew that brain trumped brawn every time.

With the slash of the referee's hand, Uno dashed across the Octagon and dealt Penn a flying round kick. Probably not a smart move, but his stomping ground was the rings of Japan, where the crowd liked a spectacle. The kick failed to hit its mark. Penn slipped aside and then retaliated with a powerful right hand to Uno's face. One of Uno's legs buckled beneath him as he dropped unconscious to the canvas. Penn wasn't finished, however. He came down on top of his foe and dismantled Uno with power bombs until the referee pulled him off. It was all over in eleven seconds.

Although I was sitting safely outside the cage, I felt as if I'd been punched—literally knocked backwards in my seat. In just eleven seconds, Penn had destroyed one of the best fighters in the world. It took me a moment to realize that my fellow commentators were talking to me, and that my voice was still being broadcast to homes around the globe. Struggling to sound professional and happy for the winner, I told the world that I wasn't worried about facing Penn to defend my title, but I just kept thinking, "Is he really that good? Is he really that damn good?"

For the first time in years, I felt a rush of fear. I had left my father's home ten years and two thousand miles behind me, yet I could still hear his voice saying, "This guy is too good, too strong, and too fast for a worthless piece of shit like you. On worldwide pay-per-view, he's going to stomp your ass—you'll see. That belt doesn't mean a thing. He's gonna take it from you, and then you'll be nothing all over again."

Because of the shocking manner in which Penn had beaten Uno, there was a lot of hype leading up to our fight. I was undefeated in the Octagon, the reigning lightweight champion of the world, and in the previous two years there hadn't been a single competitor who'd come close to knocking me off my throne. But out of nowhere, B. J. Penn had appeared, and overnight he became the new UFC poster boy. Having spent less than ten minutes in the Octagon, he'd racked up three impressive knockouts. He seemed unstoppable. Many people were calling our bout the fight of the year, much to the satisfaction of the UFC brass. They decided to make the bout the first lightweight main event in UFC history.

When I returned to Iowa after UFC XXXIV, I jumped right back into training and tried to clear my thoughts. But every time I heard B. J. Penn's name or saw his victory mentioned on the Internet, my fear grew. Once again, I had two people living inside me. They both talked to me at night as I lay in bed. The proud voice, the one that had carried me through the Seattle ghetto and all the way to Iowa, told me that this fight was no different from all the rest—if I concentrated on training, on perfecting my skills, I would be victorious. The other voice, however—the one I thought I'd finally silenced years ago—kept tearing down my confidence.

I pushed through the weeks, turning every grappling session at Miletich Fighting Systems into a war. Although I worked on how to escape arm bars, chokes, and leg locks, I didn't study any of Penn's fights. If I was going to win, I had to impose my own will and game plan. I was going to bring the fight to him and make him wish he'd never entered the Octagon with Little Evil.

Then, just as my confidence started to rally, I was dealt a devastating blow. Monte Cox told me that the Las Vegas bookies had set the odds for my fight: I was a three-to-one underdog. "What?" I shouted. "What are they looking at? Did anyone see my last six fights?"

To others, only my rage was visible. Inside, however, that sinister voice was saying, "You see! They know what's going to happen. They know who you are and what a fucking little failure you've always been. You might as well quit now—just tuck your tail between your legs and run before it's too late."

As the days passed, I began to hear the buzz about the fight. Most people were convinced that Penn was going to turn me into chopped liver. They thought he was too good for me on the ground, and too good standing. They were certain I'd be helpless against him. Penn himself was quoted as saying that he was superior to me in every way, and that if the fight went to the ground, it would be over in an instant.

I tried to look at the situation as positively as I could. If fight fans really thought that some up-and-comer nicknamed "the Prodigy" was going to knock me off my throne that easily, then I still had some proving to do. This was my chance to solidify my reputation as one of the best fighters around. It was also my greatest chance to fail.

18

Fight Night

As I bustle through the Mohegan Sun Casino in Uncasville, Connecticut, B. J. Penn is all around me. His face glares at me from posters plastered on the walls. I can hear fight fans uttering his name over the racket of slot machines. They're talking about his lightning-fast punches and stealthy ground game. I block it all out and follow my trainer, Pat Miletich, who is leading me to the locker room.

Moving through smoke-filled air, we pass roulette and blackjack tables. Then we walk down a narrow corridor and into the Mohegan Sun's arena. As my feet carry me steadily forward, I look to my right and see the Octagon surrounded by twenty thousand empty seats. My teeth clamp shut and a frown twists my face. That is my cage, my home, and I won't let anyone take it away from me! If Penn wants my title belt, then he'll have to go to hell to get it!

In the locker room, I strip off my street clothes and put on my fighting trunks. Then I wait, and the hours dissolve in a whirl of emotions. My brother Abel comes in and sits beside me. Having him so close reminds me of my youth. One moment, I'm smiling, picturing the three Pulver boys running loose on the Backside. The next moment, every muscle in by body tightens as I think about how my mother was forced to raise us on food stamps and state aid. I experience every emotion known to man, and I feel glad that Abel is here for me.

At one point during those confusing hours, Abel taps me on the shoulder, drawing me out of my delirium. He hands me a sealed envelope. It's a letter from Dustin—I recognize his handwriting. He has written to me from prison, sending his love and good wishes. I read the letter over and over again. His gesture makes me realize that this fight isn't just for me.

Then Miletich tells me it's time to start my warm-up. I stand, shake off my emotions, and begin to throw long, stretched-out punches at the focus mitts. Each time my hand connects, my anger swells. Who does Penn think he is, walking around saying he's going to beat me? Who are those sons of bitches in Las Vegas setting the odds? And what about those motherfuckers talking trash on the Internet, saying Penn is too good for me on the ground, and too good standing up?

Sweat beads on my brow. Matt Hughes steps in and pulls me down to the mat. We drill takedowns and sprawls. He climbs into the mount, and I shake him off. My heart is pounding in my chest. I practice one submission after another, mentally preparing myself for a twenty-five-minute war.

Someone else enters the dressing room—it's Leon Tabs, the world-famous cut man, here to wrap my hands. After he winds a length of tape around my knuckles, I open and close my fist and smack it a few times against the opposite palm so I can feel the power. My hands are going to win this fight. They're going to draw blood.

Leon wishes me luck and leaves. A member of the production crew comes to tell me that I've got five minutes. It's time to get focused. Time to reach down into the depths of my soul and pull up the warrior. I close my eyes, and as Pat Miletich rubs grease on my face, I hear my fellow teammates, one by one, tell me that they love me. Then it's time to go.

I follow Pat with my head down, my eyes pinned to the floor. We move through corridors and around corners. Finally, we start to ascend a very familiar flight of stairs. I have never fought at the Mohegan Sun before, but I still know these stairs. They lead up to the future, to victory or defeat. There are only twenty of them, at most, but they always feel a thousand miles long, and they take an eternity to climb. They are magical in many ways. On them, time stands still, reminding me of my mortality.

As I climb, one foot after the other, I begin to sense the crowd. Its voice thumps in my chest, its heat pushes against me. Someone is blowing an air horn, and someone else is shouting, "I want to see some blood!" But above the racket, a voice is speaking to me. I can't tell if it's coming from the crowd or from inside my own head. It could merely be a figment of my imagination, a memory tunneling up from the past. In my altered mental state, the only thing I'm certain of is that the voice belongs to my father.

He tells me what he always tells me: I'm going to fail. Although I haven't been listening in the past couple of years, I now realize that the voice has always been here, on this flight of stairs and on others just like it. It's a pressure on the back of my brain, a pressure that only winning can relieve. Before I can reach the top step, I am once again trapped inside my father's terrible world. My only means of escape is my fists. Victory is my only chance for temporary salvation.

The next few minutes are a blur, a dream in which I'm wandering through a dense fog and hands pop out of nowhere. My name echoes all around, and camera lenses zero in on my face. Nothing makes sense until I see the cage sitting beneath a halo of light. That's when my mind clears and I emerge from the fog.

Inside the Octagon, referee John McCarthy lays out the rules for us. I nod my head and glare across at B. J. the Terrible, the Prodigy, the fighting sensation from Hawaii. He's bouncing around, trying to stare me down. I feel nothing—no fear, no tension. I have left my emotions behind in the locker room, on the staircase. Focusing all of my attention on the referee, I watch his lips move and listen for the words that will begin the fight.

"Let's get it on!" he bellows.

I move forward, and when I have Penn within striking distance, I let my left jab fly. I'm eager to draw blood. I see it all in slow motion. Just before my knuckles collide with Penn's face, his head drops out of sight. He, too, wants to end this quickly, and he's going for the takedown.

No fear. Over the months leading up to this bout, I've drilled thousands of sprawls and avoided the takedowns of some of the world's best shooters. Once my legs are kicked back, my weight will come crashing down on my opponent. I'll pin him beneath me and slam his kidneys with one hook after another.

My legs are kicked back, but something is wrong. I'm not crashing down. Suddenly I feel Penn's arms wrapping around my hamstrings, his shoulders driving into my hips. Before I can react, he hauls me down on my back. As Penn scrambles on top of me, I think, "He really *is* fast!" I push the thought out of my mind—this is no time to be marveling at my opponent's abilities. Any second now, he'll start hunting for submissions, and I need to remain calm in order to avoid them. Keep your arms in, hold your head straight, be aware of his hips: this is my game plan, the survival method that Miletich has burned into my brain. It doesn't matter that I didn't get to punch a hole in Penn's face. We're on the ground now, and I'm going to make the best of it. Penn's past victories don't matter—it wasn't me he knocked out in the first round, and it wasn't me he competed against in Brazil during the world jiu-jitsu championships. This is the Octagon, my fucking home.

Penn's hands begin to probe my body, looking for a dangling limb. I shove them away and chop at his ribs, searching for an opening so I can get back to my feet. The seconds tick down in my head, and when sixty of them have gone by, I manage to wedge my feet under Penn's hips and give him a massive push. I watch as his body soars away, making an instantaneous decision to jump to my feet. It's a dangerous move, because if he recovers his balance first, then he can drop a knee to my face or go for a choke.

Just as the soles of my feet touch the canvas, Penn's body comes hurtling back at me. He wraps his legs around my waist and his right arm around my head. Carrying all of his weight, I stagger to keep my balance. I can feel his forearm cinching my neck. If I fall, the fight may be over. I know that Penn's hold will get tighter and tighter until black dots swim across my field of vision and I lose consciousness. I'll wake up on my back to witness his hand being raised in the air.

I tell myself to stay calm. I know how to avoid this. During daily practices when I first arrived in Iowa, I fell victim to countless choke holds. Trained as a wrestler, I was used to shooting in blindly, leaving my neck exposed. But I don't do that anymore. I haven't been caught in a guillotine in over a year. I avoid it by staying calm. Thinking. Breathing.

My hand rises and finds Penn's elbow. I push the elbow up until he's forced to peel his arm off my head. Air rushes into my lungs, but I'm not out of the woods yet. His legs are still around me, and he's clinging tight. Although my options aren't extensive, one good one is still available. I take three steps forward and then leap into the air. Penn takes the fall with me, and as we hit the canvas I hear his lungs compress. He immediately covers his head to protect it from my blows. I have demonstrated my power. I've surprised him. He thought he was going to make me his bitch on the ground, but now he's lying on his back, the wind sucked out of him.

I begin my assault, punching his body and head. My ear is pressed to his chest, and I can hear my shots echoing in his guts. I'm hurting him, but I have to be careful, because Penn is a sleeping dragon. He's waiting for me to leave an arm exposed. I can feel him moving beneath me, continually searching.

It goes on like this for the remainder of this round and the beginning of the next. A chess match. Both of us play it cool until an opportunity to strike presents itself. Penn keeps taking me down, looking for a submission, but I keep finding my way back to my feet. We go up and down, up and down, but with just two minutes left in the second round, when I'm starting to feel like I can ride this one home, Penn spots an opportunity. Taking me to the canvas, he scoots effortlessly around my legs and climbs into the mount.

My heart skips a beat. With his weight bearing down on me, Penn sees a hundred opportunities opening before him. Although my opponent is an arm-bar specialist and it would be easy for him to find a submission in this position, that's not what worries me. I'm

179

worried about his striking. I tell myself, "Don't let him flurry. Do whatever you must to stop the flurry." If he begins to land shots and McCarthy thinks the abuse is too severe, the fight will be called. To avoid such a devastating outcome, I reach up and grip Penn's head, pulling it onto my chest. Once I have him under control, I glance over to my corner to check the time. Less than two minutes remaining. I can hold on for two minutes.

Every time Penn breaks free, I buck with all my might, trying to bring him back down so I can cling to him. But he's a snake. He slithers away from my grasp, then he begins throwing blows. A few just graze my chin, and I look to McCarthy to let him know I'm still in the fight. The ref's eyes are squinting, watching Penn's every move. I need to do something, and I need to do it fast.

I give Penn my arm, just like that, and he swings around for an arm bar, just as I'd anticipated. Immediately, I block the arm bar by rising up, but then Penn blocks me by slipping back into the mount. Same dangerous position, only now there is less than a minute left. I try everything. I hold him down. Buck. Wedge my feet up into his armpits. But, despite all my efforts, disaster occurs with just five seconds left.

Before I can even sense his movement, Penn snatches my arm for a second time and swings around to lock it out. I've been counting down the seconds in my mind, and I know I only have to last a moment longer. Instead of trying to escape, I lock my hands together with all of my strength, sure that he doesn't have enough time to break my hold.

Just as the buzzer sounds, I let my hands slip apart and straighten my arm. The round is over, and Penn should let go, but he doesn't. He's still trying to break my arm, and anger boils up inside me. I punch his leg, screaming, "Get off my fucking arm!"

After McCarthy breaks up the action, I get to my feet, cursing under my breath. The anger is gone, however, by the time I reach my corner. Having narrowly escaped defeat, I experience a rush of doubt. In my mind, I replay the entire fight to this moment, and I honestly can't see how I'm going to beat Penn. He's been taking me down at will, mounting me with ease, and if it hadn't been for the buzzer, he might very well have ended the fight with an arm bar. "Jesus," I think, "there's no fucking way I can win this fight. There's nothing I can do to stop this guy."

My trainer Jeremy Horn shouts, "Be ready for the sprawl! You're hurting him with those punches, and he's scared of you!" I'm not listening to him, however. All I can think about is how I'm going to lose, and just as I begin picturing the worst—tapping out due to some ridiculous toe hold—I spot a spectator in the crowd behind Penn's corner men who's mocking me. He's slitting his throat with a finger, telling me I'm done. I can't take my eyes off him, and all at once my anger returns. There is no way I'm going to give that son of a bitch the satisfaction of being right. What does Penn have on me, anyway? Even if he shoots in,

I'm a better wrestler. What's the worst thing that could happen? I could get mounted again, but I've already been there. He just had me mounted, and he couldn't finish me.

At the opening of the third round, I turn on the juice, and I don't turn it off until the end of the fight. I come out with jab-cross combinations, looking to take his head off. Although the fight starts going up and down again, I've become more familiar with Penn's takedowns, and I consistently come out on top. When I get there, I beat on his ribs and face before escaping back to my feet. Landing one punch after another, I chop Penn's confidence down to the point where he stops shooting in altogether.

By the fifth round, I've forced Penn to abandon his game plan and the bout turns into a full-out, stand-up war. Despite Penn's knockout history, he can't hang with me on his feet. I slam his face with countless punches, and although he lands his fair share, it becomes evident to the thousands in attendance and the millions watching at home that the Octagon is my domain. I want the knockout so bad I can taste it, but even though I'm laying it all on the line, Penn digs deep and manages to weather the storm. Once again, my future is in the hands of the three judges.

I return to my corner, exhausted. My trainers assure me that I've won, but I don't want to get my hopes up. In the third round I had gone wild, dominating every minute. But Penn had made an impression during the opening rounds, and you never know what will stick in the judges' minds. All I can do is hope. But no matter what happens, I know I'll never feel disappointed in the way I've performed here tonight. I have given 100 percent—which, I'm starting to learn, is all we can ever give.

We return to the center of the ring. I stand to McCarthy's right, Penn to his left. Announcer Bruce Buffer speaks into the microphone. The moment I hear him say, "And the winner, by majority decision, and *still* . . . ," all the emotions I had pushed aside before the fight come rushing back.

After months of being ripped apart, of reading negative press, of listening to Penn boast about his superiority, of going to sleep to the sound of my father's voice, I have emerged victorious. The three-to-one underdog has proven everyone wrong. I have defended my belt against the top prospect, and I truly feel like a champion.

As the cameras hone in on me, I look out at the world, and I finally have the courage to tell the truth. I say, "B. J. Penn wasn't anything. After getting beat on all my life by my old man, there isn't anything I can't handle."

For the first time in my life, I know that this is the truth.

19

Revelations

There was a time when my father could ride like the wind and inspire a crowd of thousands to give a thunderous roar. I remember watching him when I was very young, before the demons worked their way into his heart. He was the envy of many, and a hero to most. Sitting in the stands at Long Acres, I was in awe of this proud and confident man who swept past me on his powerful horse like an ocean wave. He was larger than Long Acres, greater than all the tracks in the country. He was my father, and I never doubted that he was in complete control of his destiny.

Back then, however, I was too young to see what the racetrack meant to my father. It wasn't his love or passion. It was his church—the only place where he could find salvation. The beating of his horse's hooves resounded in his chest as he raced not towards glory, but away from fear. Still, no matter how hard or fast or long he rode, he couldn't escape the nightmares that waited for him. They were there in the silence of his bedroom, in his wife's embrace, in his children's faces.

The warmth in his life brought him only darkness, and he soon grew tired of trying to outrun it.

My father forced me to watch him fall to ruins. He forced me to watch him degenerate until the only thing he had left to offer was pain. He forced me to learn from his own cowardly existence, and that, above all, made me hate him.

Even after I had achieved glory in the Octagon, I couldn't help but wonder if the fate my father had suffered would be mine as well. Perhaps one day I'd find myself drugged out, sleeping in a Seattle garage. Maybe the chemicals in the methamphetamines I consumed would raise blisters all over my body and my insides would be destroyed by hepatitis. This is what happened to my father. I wondered if, towards the end, as he put another batch of crank on the burner, he could still hear his name triumphantly announced to the throngs at Long Acres or Portland Meadows. Or maybe he only heard the voice of his own drunken father.

I had to wonder, not because I had any love left to give him, but because a part of me remained frightened. My father's lessons were deeply ingrained in me, and for years I had been trying to scrub them off by chasing victory after victory. By doing so—by trying desperately to bury the past—I was following the very path my father had taken.

I spent a few hard weeks after successfully defending my title struggling to see the future, failing to understand that revelations don't just fall into your lap—you have to earn them. Once the thrill of my victory over B. J. Penn had begun to fade, I thought long and hard about the road I had walked in the previous two years. I realized that it wasn't the road I'd assumed it was; I had gotten waylaid some time ago. I think it happened when I left Boise and returned to Seattle to attend junior college. Although I'd told myself I was going home to conquer old demons, that was a lie. I had gone back to awaken those demons. In trying to confront and eradicate aspects of my past, I'd actually been embracing them.

Certain facts of my life I'd never be able to change, no matter how hard I tried to conquer them. Like the fact that as a child I'd often heard my mother scream my name in the middle of the night as my father laid into her with his fists. Like the fact that my brother had shot a man and was now in prison.

But I did manage to make peace with some of the hard truths of my life during my two-year stint in Seattle, and that gave me strength. I had harnessed my deep-rooted infatuation with fear and pain, and I used it to my advantage. I may have spent the first twelve years of my life in hell, but now I knew that I could handle the heat, and that gave me an advantage not only in the ring, but also in life. The demons were still there—they weren't ever going to go away—but if they wanted to dance, I'd dance twice as hard, until they quit.

If only my father had achieved a similar revelation, then he might still be riding horses competitively. Perhaps he would have become a world champion, like his son, recalling how his past had almost defeated him. Of course, that's not the way things worked out. I guess some people are like Dusty—they die long before they achieve their dreams; and others are like my father— they die long before their date with death. And then there are those, like me, who are given many chances to find the right path.

Russ Hayden was right on the money when he said that everyone and everything has its time and place. Right now, my place is on top of the mountain, but even if I fall off, I have the feeling that I'll be just fine.